David Mohrhardt and Richard E. Schinkel

• STACKPOLE BOOKS •

To my father, Edmund Schinkel,

who allowed me the freedom to explore

Published by
STACKPOLE BOOKS
Cameron and Kelker Streets
P.O. Box 1831
Harrisburg, PA 17105

Printed in the United States of America

10 9 8 7 6 5 4 3 2 1

First Edition

Cover and interior illustrations by David Mohrhardt
Cover design by Tracy Patterson with Caroline Miller
Interior design by Tracy Patterson
Typesetting and Graphic composition by ART UNLIMITED

Library of Congress Cataloging-in-Publication Data

Mohrhardt, David
   Suburban Nature Guide: how to discover and identify the wildlife in your backyard/David Mohrhardt and Richard E. Schinkel.—1st ed.
   p. cm.
   Includes bibliographical references.
   ISBN 0-8117-3080-8
   1. Animals—Identification—Popular works. 2. Plants—Identification—Popular works. I. Schinkel, Richard E. II. Title
   QL50.M63 1991   90-10237
   591—dc20   CIP

CONTENTS

INTRODUCTION

Every day we encounter nature in our backyards. We look out the window and see the grass we have to mow, the trees that give us shade, the flowers we've planted, some birds and perhaps the occasional squirrel. But there is much more waiting to be discovered. A backyard teems with living creatures: insects like butterflies, bees, bugs, and beetles, small mammals like shrews, moles, and chipmunks, a wide variety of birds, and myriad plants—vines, shrubs, mosses, ferns, fungi, and tiny flowering weeds.

This book describes these organisms so that you can identify and come to appreciate them. It covers species that are considered wild but are commonly found in populated areas throughout the eastern United States (east of the Mississippi River). As you become familiar with your backyard wildlife, you'll begin to recognize the same species along roadsides and streams and in forests and meadows.

I've included descriptions of preferred habitats, ranges, feeding habits, and life cycles to help you know where to look for specific animals and plants. For some species I've also given tips on how to attract them to your yard, or—in the case of garden and house pests—to get rid of them if you so desire.

Suburban Nature Guide is not exhaustive, though you'll find it covers all the species that are likely to frequent suburban areas. Rather it's a first step, an introduction to the infinite variety of plants and animals that surrounds us. For instance, after reading this you may be interested in a field guide just on birds or wildflowers, so a list of specialized reference books is given in the bibliography.

In today's world we are becoming more and more concerned about our environment. In order to do away with anything that might endanger it, such as pollution, global warming, and the extinction of species, we must first learn to fully appreciate it. Our backyards are a great place to start. After learning about the habits and life cycles of the creatures there we can broaden our perspectives to include the nature and wildlife we encounter beyond our neighborhoods.

It is only with an appreciation of the wildlife around us that we can hope to keep our planet and environment intact and healthy. I hope this suburban nature guide will become a stepping stone for your enjoyment of the entire out-of-doors.

Dick Schinkel
Berrien Springs, Michigan

CHAPTER • ONE

MAMMALS

Mammals make their homes in a variety of ways in our yards. Trees provide homes for squirrels, bats, raccoons, opossums, and sometimes mice. Other mammals make their homes underground. A few, such as the eastern cottontail rabbit, may spend much of their lives in the open retreating to holes or brush piles in extreme cold or danger.

Although most mammals are not dangerous, caution should be used around any animal, even more so if the animal can be approached unnaturally closely. Mammals have sharp teeth and nails and can inflict serious injury.

Red Squirrel
page 93

This common small squirrel has a reddish gray back and a white belly. A black stripe separates the two colors. Adults are between ten and fourteen inches long including the tail. Sometimes called "piny" or "chickaree," this little squirrel chatters noisily at any disturbance. Red squirrels live underground, in trees, or in buildings. Usually four to six young are born in the spring and a second litter arrives in the fall.

The red squirrel can be a welcome addition to the yard and provide great enjoyment. To some it can also be a source of irritation, however, eating bird food and feeders alike. Many people who feed birds in their yards provide a separate feeder for squirrels containing sunflower or corn. This prevents damage to the other bird feeders and allows many pleasurable hours watching the squirrels. During seasons when food is abundant, this animal "squirrels" away extra seeds, nuts, and mushrooms.

Eastern Gray Squirrel

The two color phases of the eastern gray squirrel are black and gray. Many towns want black-phase squirrels protected because of their rarity. Both col-

Eastern Grey Squirrel, continued

ors may be born to the same female. In the summer the gray squirrel has a brownish tawny color on its back and sides. The tail is very bushy and has white tips on the outer hairs. The gray squirrel is larger than the red, measuring between sixteen and twenty inches. Three to five young are born in early spring, naked and blind. Usually two litters are born each year.

Truly a squirrel of the trees, the gray squirrel rarely travels on the ground unless it is burying nuts. Usually it moves from tree to tree by racing and leaping across the high branches. In the absence of trees, power lines and poles work well as highways to the next neighborhood. The gray squirrel is great fun to watch but may cause problems at bird feeding stations.

Eastern Fox Squirrel
page 93

Although predominantly a forest or forest-edge squirrel, the eastern fox squirrel can also be found in backyards throughout most of the eastern United States with the exception of New England (the northern part of Pennsylvania up to Maine). This squirrel is a foxy red with a large bushy tail. It usually ranges in length from twenty to twenty-two inches, though fox squirrels in the southern range tend to be a bit smaller. The eastern fox squirrel spends more time on the ground than do the gray and red squirrels. It prefers to feed upon nuts and berries as they fall to the ground instead of taking them from the trees.

Eastern fox squirrels have adapted very well to suburban life and often come to bird feeders and squirrel feeders. They have also adapted to the edges along farm land, especially where corn is grown. They like to hide nuts and berries underground and locate and devour them during the winter. They find the buried food either by smell or by remembering where it is hidden.

The fox squirrel usually has two litters per year. The first mating occurs in late winter and three to

Eastern Fox Squirrel, continued

five young are born. The second brood is usually born in mid to late summer. The young usually are weaned and able to leave the nest at ten to twelve weeks of age. During the summer the fox squirrel makes a nest of leaves at the tops of trees. It may or may not bear its young there. Most often the young are born in a den tree, especially if it is the first litter.

During the winter fox squirrels sleep in dens in hollow trees or nest boxes that people put out for them. They are not a serious pest to bird feeders, although they will chew them trying to get at the food. Many people provide additional food for them, such as ears of corn, which they seem to prefer over most other birdseed. You can deter the squirrels by placing baffles both above and below your feeders. Watching the squirrels trying to get at your feeders can be well worth the effort and expense of feeding.

Flying Squirrel
page 93

Flying squirrels are the smallest and least known of our squirrels. Few people have seen them because they are nocturnal and quite secretive. Their fur is a soft, pale grayish brown on the back, gray on the sides with a dark line along the gliding skin fold, and creamy white on the underside. The tail is quite bushy but can be flattened when used as a rudder during the squirrel's gliding flight. Probably the most noticeable feature of the flying squirrel is its large, prominent black eyes. These animals are only nine to eleven inches long (including the tail).

Flying squirrels prefer older neighborhoods and parks containing mature hardwoods that provide nuts and seeds. They like to visit bird feeders at night and are especially fond of sunflower seeds. This almost wholly nocturnal animal is quite pretty and is welcome in any backyard situation. Although flying squirrels are cute and can be nice pets, it is best to obtain them from licensed breeders as it is illegal to take them from the wild.

Flying squirrel boxes or bluebird houses may be used for nesting in areas lacking natural nest cavities. Two broods of two to six young are normally produced each year. The spring litter is usually born from mid April through June and the fall litter as late as October. It takes an extensive period, about nine to ten weeks, for the mother to wean the young. Nuts, seeds, and berries make up the bulk of this squirrel's food supply, but during the spring and summer, buds, insects, and baby birds supplement their diet. The flying squirrel is probably the most voracious of the squirrels when it comes to eating other living things.

The flying squirrel does not really fly. It glides downward on two folds of skin from one spot to another. These squirrels can achieve great distances quietly and effortlessly. Horizontal distances exceeding fifty feet have been recorded.

The most common sound heard from the flying squirrel is a high-pitched squeak much like that of a baby bird. This is usually an alarm call. If you imitate a screech owl call at night and hear such a squeak, it indicates the presence of flying squirrels.

Thirteen-lined Ground Squirrel
page 93

Though it is not a gopher, the thirteen-lined ground squirrel is often called this in many parts of the eastern United States. Instead of the thirteen lines we would expect to see, there are actually twenty-three stripes, twelve dark brown and eleven creamy white. The stripes do not continue onto the head as they do on the chipmunk. When running, the ground squirrel extends its tail parallel to the ground, as opposed to the chipmunk whose tail sticks straight up. At eight to twelve inches, it is a bit larger than the chipmunk. The ground squirrel lives in holes in the ground and likes grassy areas, not forests. It is a true hibernator, venturing out in March or April. Seven to ten young are born in early summer.

Ground squirrels are basically beneficial animals and the slight damage they do with their digging is outweighed by the numerous insects they eat, such as grubs. They also eat seeds and store them in their burrows. If thirteen-lined ground squirrels become a nuisance in the garden or yard, they can easily be trapped using peanut butter as bait.

Chipmunk
page 93

The chipmunk is a favorite backyard mammal. Chipmunks have stripes on their heads as well as on their sides and backs. The white stripes are set off by black or dark brown borders. The side and back stripes extend only to the rump. Chipmunks measure between seven and eleven inches long.

These animals like areas with trees, so if your yard is devoid of large trees you will probably not have chipmunks. Their nests are in holes in the ground for the most part. In these tunnels, which may extend twelve feet or more, the chipmunk stores food, sleeps, and raises its young. Although the chipmunk is an opportunist when feeding, it prefers seeds, nuts, and berries.

Two to eight young are born in early May and leave the den burrow and their parents by early June. A second batch of young is born in early fall. Although we may see more than one chipmunk at a bird feeder, they are normally solitary animals and aggressively defend their territory.

Not usually considered a nuisance, this beautiful little mammal is amusing to watch as it scurries about, filling its pouches and storing food. The chipmunk lives off its cache of stored seeds and nuts during the winter, going into resting stages off and on but not actually hibernating. Even in the dead of winter the chipmunk may dig its way out of the frozen ground and snow to visit our feeders and gather seed.

Eastern Cottontail Rabbit
page 94

The cottontail is probably the best known and most easily recognized of all the mammals in our yards. We can usually find a cottontail somewhere in the

Eastern Cottontail Rabbit, continued

neighborhood even though they are most active at night and during hours of low light. The cottontail rabbit is brownish gray above with a white or off-white belly and a cottony white tail. Adults are anywhere from fourteen to twenty inches long.

The cottontail is perfectly adapted to our suburban way of life. It thrives on habitat that is a mixture of trees, shrubs, and open areas. Throw in a well cultivated garden and the cottontail is living in luxury.

Three to five babies are born in March. As many as four litters can occur per year, and the females of the earliest litter are able to breed by the end of the summer. Before giving birth the female finds a depression or digs a hollow in the ground just a few inches deep and lines it with grass and fur from her own belly. This nest is usually well concealed although it may be right in our rose garden or lawn. To nurse the young bunnies, the female lies over the top of the nest while the young suckle. This nursing may be done several times during the day and night. The young, although quite small, are ready to leave in three to four weeks. It is during this time that we come across young rabbits that are only five to six inches long and think they must be orphaned. If they are out of the nest, the best thing you can do is release them in your yard or in a place as safe from dogs and cats as possible.

Cottontails are a welcome addition to our yard provided no damage to gardens or ornamental plantings occurs. Today there are a number of ways rabbits can be controlled without harming them. For non-food plants a substance called RO-PEL, which can be put directly on the plants, works very well. For edible plants, fencing is probably the surest way to keep the rabbits out. For the latest ways to control garden pests contact your county agricultural extension agent.

Spotted Skunk
page 94

Mainly found in the southern part of the eastern United States, this small skunk has a black and white

Spotted Skunk,
continued

pattern consisting of broken stripes and spots. The tail usually has a white tip and the head is black, with white spots near the ears and cheeks. Color variations do occur and an animal may show more black or more white. Full-grown spotted skunks vary in size from sixteen to twenty-four inches.

The four to six young are usually born in May and are able to forage for themselves in about two months. It is a beneficial animal because of the great amount of insects it eats. Its main diet is fruit, insects, and mice, which can all usually be found in our yards. Their presence can cause problems like the spraying of pets and scattering of trash. This skunk lives in burrows and rock piles so the elimination of home sites can keep visitations to a minimum.

Striped Skunk
page 94

This large skunk, measuring between twenty-two and twenty-nine inches, may be found throughout the eastern United States and is easily identified by its jet black fur and the white stripes on its face, neck, back, and usually its tail. As with the spotted skunk, a wide range of color variations can occur.

The striped skunk has readily adapted to the suburban way of life, eating everything from garbage to insects to garden vegetables. The skunk likes to live under buildings and porches, in holes in the ground, or any place of safe haven.

Four to six young are born in April or May and are able to spray musk as soon as they have fur and their eyes are open. This ability to spray is often a source of distress to those who have found baby skunks that have wandered into their basement or garage.

The striped skunk and the spotted skunk are very nearsighted and slow. Their nocturnal habits usually help them avoid human contact, but occasionally the family dog or cat — or even an unlucky member of the family — may have a brief but disastrous encounter. Several commercial remedies are available through pet shops and vets to rid pets and

**Striped Skunk,
continued**

clothing of the musk smell. Some old home reme- dies that have some value are tomato juice, ammo- nia, and vinegar. Dry cleaning does some good but usually repeated treatments are necessary.

In the last couple of years the skunk has become more prominent as a pet. Although they can be as cute and playful as kittens, some care should be taken. It is illegal to take a skunk from the wild. Only skunks bred in captivity are legal, and of course shots and immunizations are mandatory, especially those for rabies and distemper.

Though probably not as beneficial as the spotted skunk, the striped skunk does eat many insects, especially those near the surface of the ground. It also has a taste for garden fruit and vegetables. Although it does not technically hibernate, the striped skunk spends much of the winter sleeping, only becoming active during warm sunny days as spring progresses.

Raccoon
page 94

The raccoon has adapted to man's existence proba- bly better than any other suburban mammal. It is easily recognizable by the "bandit" black mask and the alternating rings of dark and light gray on its tail. The body color can be anywhere from a light silvery gray to almost black. Raccoons are larger than many dogs; adults measure between twenty- five and forty inches.

The raccoon is extremely adept at finding avail- able food sources in our neighborhoods. It has learned to use dog and cat entrances to our homes, open garbage cans, and raid bird feeders. Campers have often discovered, much to their dismay, the ability of raccoons to steal into trailers and tents and haul away packs and foodstuff. Once a food source has been found, it is difficult to rid yourself of these persistent bandits.

Raccoons spend the winter months sleeping and conserving energy. They only become active during mild periods. Four to seven young are born in late

March, April, and May. These births are usually our first encounter of the year with the animals. Often "Mom" has her babies in the chimney and the young start making noises. Closing the chimney damper and waiting out the spring is the easiest solution. If you must get rid of the raccoons, sometimes a heavily soaked ammonia rag placed in the chimney at night will prompt the family to relocate. Either way, once the raccoons are gone, a critter-proof cap should be placed on top of the chimney, or they'll be back. In early summer the young begin to follow the mother in her nightly excursions for food. The antics of the young at a feeding station are enjoyable and well worth the grief these animals sometimes give.

Raccoons can become quite tame, but they must always be regarded as wild animals. If they become a pest, live trapping and relocating them a long distance away (at least ten to twenty miles) is the best solution. Be sure to check with local game authorities for permits and regulations regarding trapping. Raccoons can make good pets, but as with skunks, wild raccoons cannot be used. Only those that come from a licensed breeder with their proper shots and immunizations are legal.

Opossum
page 94

This cat-sized mammal of our backyards is a marsupial, the only marsupial (meaning pouched) animal in North America. The opossum has a prehensile, or monkeylike, naked tail. Opossums can get fairly large, measuring from twenty-seven to thirty-two inches and sometimes weighing more than ten pounds. The opossum has gray fur with an almost white underfur. Its face resembles that of a large rat. In addition to the bald tail, the toes, nose, and long ears also lack fur. In the northern parts of North America, this can be quite distressing to the opossum. Frequently you may find opossums with ears, toes, and tail frostbitten or even missing. Despite this major hindrance, the opossum is expanding its range from the south to the cold north.

The life of this marsupial is truly amazing. The opossum mates in early spring and the nine to eighteen young are born in only thirteen days. At this age, all the young would fit into a tablespoon. They must then crawl on their own to the mother's pouch where they attach themselves to one of the thirteen to eighteen nipples. The journey of a few inches to the pouch is not achieved by all the babies; even if they do make it, some won't find a place for nourishment. Generally six to ten young emerge from the mother's pouch in about two months. The young then begin to feed with the mother and spend the next couple of months following her on nightly journeys.

This marsupial can live anywhere in your neighborhood that can give shelter and food, such as under a porch, in a tree, or in a culvert. An opossum literally eats anything. A Wisconsin study done on the stomachs of road-killed opossums revealed such items as balloons, bottle caps, rubber bands, and plastic bags. During the winter the opossum will even eat birdseed.

"Playing possum" is one way this animal survives. Its initial tactic upon encountering a threat is to run away. If caught it turns and bares its fifty teeth, hissing and growling. Upon further encounter, the opossum feigns death, becoming semi-curled and rigid with its lips curled back as if dried, and showing its teeth. While in this state the opossum can be moved with no signs of life, not even flinching or blinking. Many animals, uninterested in pursuing a dead animal, will leave it alone. After being left a short time (ten to twenty minutes) the opossum wakes up and rambles off.

Eastern Mole
page 95

Although not often seen, this mammal makes its presence known by its network of raised earth tunnels. The eastern mole has soft, dark gray fur that does not lie in any particular direction. It has a hair-

Eastern Mole,
continued

less nose, tail, and feet, small black eyes, and ears that are barely visible. The mole is easily identified by these characteristics. It is between five and eight inches long.

Usually four young are born once a year in April or May and leave their mother after five to six weeks. The eastern mole is a beneficial animal, although it is definitely not appreciated in well manicured lawns and gardens. The mole forages underground for grubs, worms, insects, and some plant material. It also aerates the ground with its digging. If moles become a problem, the best control is trapping the animals. Traps are available from your local garden center or hardware store (See appendix). The use of poisons is not recommended, nor is it as effective as trapping.

Star-nosed Mole
page 95

Besides having the general characteristics of the eastern mole, the star-nosed mole has twenty-two fleshy, fingerlike projections coming from its nose. Its tail is hairy and quite constricted close to the mole's body. It is larger than the eastern mole (seven to nine inches long), and the long tunnels it makes are deeper and therefore not as obvious. What are seen and recognized are the molehills it makes in the process of digging deeper burrows. These hills are tall, rounded mounds with no visible entrances or exits and can appear even during the dead of winter. The star-nosed moles prefer moist soil usually near streams and lakes.

Four to five young are born in April through May and are ready to leave the mother in four to five weeks. Again, they are beneficial except for the unsightly molehills. The star-nosed mole can also be controlled with traps. Because of its preference for wet areas, however, it is probably less of a nuisance than the eastern mole. In the past some of its fur was used in the clothing industry, but this practice is rare today.

Shrew
page 95

The shrew, although not common, can be found in most of our suburban neighborhoods, especially those near grassy or shrubby fields. One or more species of shrew can be found throughout the United States, but trying to distinguish between very similar species can be difficult. The shrew, our smallest mammal at two to five inches long, is somewhat mouselike with the exception of its small eyes, long, pointed nose, and tiny ears.

House Mouse
page 95

This common mouse of our homes and outbuildings is easily distinguished from the deer mouse because it has a nearly hairless tail and its underside is buff or gray, never white. The house mouse is a dull gray on the head and upper parts of its body and measures between six and seven inches. It eats just about anything and has adapted well to mankind around the world. It is a particular nuisance where grain is being stored, so care should be taken to mouseproof containers and buildings.

The house mouse may have as many as a dozen young per litter, but five to six is more common. They can have as many as seven to eight litters each year. Luckily, the house mouse is readily trapped in snap traps or on sticky boards. Some live traps are procurable for those who do not wish to harm the mice, but release should be a number of miles away. Traps can be baited with anything that gives off a strong odor such as tuna, cheese, bacon, or peanut butter. Unless you seal the entry points to your home, you will have a recurring problem. If left uncontrolled the house mouse can become a large colony and be quite a nuisance, chewing books, boxes, and clothing as well as eating anything in sight.

Deer Mouse and White-footed Mouse
page 95

Technically the deer mouse and white-footed mouse are different species, but because they are almost impossible to distinguish we will deal with them

**Deer Mouse and
White-footed Mouse,
continued**

together. This pretty mouse has a white belly and white feet with large, shining black eyes. It is a light brown above with usually a tan and white tail and is five to eight inches in size.

This mouse likes the forested and brushy areas of our yards, but may invade a building if the opportunity arises. Not as harmful as the house mouse, this cute animal with big ears can sometimes become the pet of a bird feeding area. The four to six young begin life in March and litters continue throughout the summer at about six to seven week intervals until cold weather sets in.

The deer mouse is a storer of seeds and may have two or three secret caches of maple or sunflower seeds put away for the winter. During the summer, insects and berries may be added to their diet of seeds. This means the deer mouse is beneficial as a controller of insects but can also become a nuisance in our berry patches.

Norway Rat
page 95

The Norway rat is a uniform grayish brown with an almost hairless scaly tail. It is a very damaging rodent. This rat usually lives in underground colonies, often under garages or outbuildings. The Norway rat is attracted to food of any kind and will chew through walls and cupboards to get to it. Since it is a carrier of diseases that can be transmitted to man, the Norway rat should be eliminated from homes. I recommend trapping, because poison allows the rat to die in a wall where the odor can become close to unbearable. Keeping food in sealed containers and closing areas of access are among the best ways to prevent reinfestation.

**Big Brown Bat or
House Bat**

Found throughout nearly the entire United States, this bat is probably the one most commonly encountered by humans. The big brown bat frequents old buildings, barns, and homes. It lives in attics, around chimneys, and even in garages. The big brown bat is dark brown all over with black ears and wing membranes.

Because it lives in close proximity to our homes and has a habit of relocating for no apparent reason, even in the winter, it often comes in direct contact with people. It is sometimes portrayed as a "bad" bat because it is large enough to bite if handled. Its body is between $3^1/2$ and $4^1/2$ inches long and it has a wingspread of eleven to thirteen inches. These bats are late-night risers and usually feed during the late night and early morning hours. Larger insects such as beetles, flies, and moths make up the greatest portion of their diet. The big brown bat feeds close to the ground, unnerving late evening walkers. A very beneficial bat, it should be encouraged to frequent our suburban neighborhoods. Usually two young are born in May or June and remain with the mother four to six weeks.

As in all insect-eating bats, the use of echolocation is important in obtaining food. Echolocation is the use of high-frequency sounds emitted by the bats to locate potential prey down to gnat size. Throw a small pebble into the air as a bat passes nearby. The bat will swoop to investigate and even catch the pebble thinking it is an insect. The bat may capture the pebble in its mouth, but most often scoops it up with its feet. After catching the pebble and discovering its inedible properties, the bat will drop it a few yards away. This process takes but an instant.

Bats are very beneficial animals. However, there are many misconceptions about them. Vampire bats, which feed on the blood of other animals, do not live in the United States. All of the eastern bats are insectivorous, or insect eating. Another misconception, that bats will get in your hair, is untrue. If they seem to be aiming for your head, it is because they are catching insects such as mosquitoes that home in on you as you walk in the evening. Their sense of echolocation is very acute, and they do not make the mistake of getting caught in people's hair.

It is also a myth that all bats carry rabies. Actually bats have a very low incidence of this disease.

Little Brown Bat
page 95

A dweller of caves, hollow trees, and sometimes even homes, the little brown bat is a pale olive brown to yellowish brown in color with a darker shoulder. It sometimes lives alongside the big brown bat and is probably the most common bat in the United States' suburbs. Nevertheless, it is seen less often than the big brown bat because of its smaller size, its habit of hibernating, and because it is not a frequent home dweller. This bat is a bit smaller than its cousin, with a body length of 3 to $3^1/2$ inches and a wing span of nine to eleven inches. It is found nearly everywhere except in the extreme southern United States. The little brown bat lives in colonies and has good homing instincts.

An early-evening riser, the little brown bat can be seen flying over ponds, lakes, and streams as well as our backyards, feeding on a multitude of insects including mosquitoes. Young are born in June or July and stay clinging to the mother three to five days before they are left alone to hang in the roost. After a month the young are able to take care of themselves.

CHAPTER TWO

BIRDS

Birds are everywhere, and bird watching is one of America's most popular pastimes. Suburbs provide many types of habitat in a small area, thus the variety of bird life is great. Habitat means food, water, and nesting sites as well as protected areas. Mature trees, shrubby areas, and open spaces are all appealing to birds.

Feeding and attracting birds is a year-round pastime and is one of the easiest ways to allow you to see and identify birds in your backyard. Begin feeding birds by placing a feeder where it can easily be seen from a comfortable, well used window. Seed used in the feeder is generally a mixture that should include sunflower, millet, and cracked corn. Many people supplement with additional sunflower seed or just feed sunflower seeds. Summer feeding will allow you to see birds not otherwise often seen, such as the colorful red-winged blackbird.

Suet (animal fat) or suet cakes placed in wire feeders attracts a variety of birds. Many birds around in the winter are insect eaters and do not eat birdseed. Suet can be used to attract these birds, especially those in the woodpecker family. Other birds that come to the suet are chickadees, titmice, nuthatches, and brown creepers. In the summer catbirds and orioles will also make good use of it.

Providing water for birds is also a great way to attract them throughout the year. More species of birds may be attracted to your yard by water than by birdseed, since all birds need water for drinking and bathing. The water in the birdbath should be no deeper than $2^1/_2$ inches. Dripping or running water also increases the likelihood that birds will use your watering area. The sound seems to draw them to it or make them notice the water.

Bird houses are another way to attract birds. They should be placed facing away from the prevailing winds and high enough that they are out of reach of small children and cats. Young birds usually leave the nest before they are able to fly well, so a small tree or shrub facing the nest box will provide them with a place to land out of harm's way. It doesn't hurt to pick the baby birds up from the ground where they might be in danger and place them out of the way in a tree or shrub. It is a myth that human scent will cause a parent bird to abandon its young or eggs. Bird houses can be obtained from your nature center, garden center, or specialty bird shop, or you may build one yourself using one of the many plan books available. The appendix at the back of this book contains instructions for building a tray feeder, an oriole feeder, a wren house, and a nesting roost. Some birds easily attracted to bird houses or roost shelves are house wrens, robins, bluebirds, barn swallows, tree swallows, chickadees, screech owls, woodpeckers, house finches, and purple martins.

Even though attracting birds is fun, birds can also become a nuisance. Keep in mind that most birds are protected in some manner by state or federal law, so problems can sometimes be tricky to eliminate without running afoul of the law. Most often it is easiest to try scaring unwanted birds away from the area. This can be done with scarecrows, dummy owls, dummy snakes, or pie tins hung by a string. Loud noises or tapes of distress or alarm calls can also be effective in scaring birds away from your garden fruits and vegetables. Timing used in scare devices is important, as constant usage allows birds to become accustomed and eventually oblivious to them. Scare tactics should be used during the period most needed, usually when fruits or vegetables are at their peak. Netting may also be purchased from garden centers to completely cover fruited areas and make them unavailable. Of course, planting extra might also be an alternative.

Another bird problem is one of selection at your feeders. For instance, how to get rid of those "nasty" blue jays? Generally, smaller birds are most success-ful at tube feeders with short perches. These selective feeders usually dispense sunflower or niger (thistle) seed. By placing your feeders closer to the viewing window, you see those birds most often. The barn style feeder will allow your bigger birds to feed without competition from the more "desirable" birds. Some manufacturers make feeders to attract birds such as cardinals, finches, and chickadees and repel birds such as jays and grackles. These feeders have small perches, which make them difficult for larger birds to use.

The birds illustrated in this book can be found in almost any backyard east of the Mississippi River. Any habitat or regional limitations will be given in the entry describing the species.

SILHOUETTES IN THE SKY

Not easily identifiable but certainly prominent are the birds that circle above our homes, usually in search of food: the predators and scavengers. Seen against the bright sky, they usually appear only as dark silhouettes. Some fre-quent suburbs because we have provided a food source for them, such as insects attracted to lights.

Red-tailed Hawk
page 96

The most common hawk of the east, the red-tailed hawk feeds mainly on small mammals and birds. It

Red-tailed Hawk, continued

measures between nineteen and twenty-six inches tall and has a wing span of about four feet. The red-tail (buzzard and chicken hawk are other common names) is easily recognized by its broad stubby wings, rusty red tail, white undersides, and dark band across the belly.

The red-tail hunts by soaring high and diving for its prey, which consist primarily of birds and small mammals. It also uses snags at the tops of trees or power line poles as high lookouts. In early spring, the red-tail puts its nest of twigs, bark, and branches high in a tree, usually near the edge of an extensive woodlot. The two to four eggs are completely white and hatch after about four weeks. The young are able to leave the nest in seven to eight weeks. Like most hawks and birds of prey it is extremely beneficial, eating lots of rodents and even insects.

American Kestrel
page 96

The American kestrel, or sparrow hawk as it is often called, is our smallest falcon and also our stockiest bird of prey. It has an oval body shape in contrast with the bullet shape of other raptors. It is seven to eight inches tall. Both male and female have cinnamon heads with bluish gray crowns, although the male's is brighter. The male has blue wings and a rust-colored tail with bars only at the end of the tail. The female is rust all over with barring on both the body and tail.

When sitting, the kestrel pumps its tail up and down. It dives from perches to seize its prey or hovers over open areas looking for food in the grass. It eats mainly grasshoppers and insects during the summer and fall and mice through the rest of the year. An easy bird to attract to suburban yards, the kestrel nests in tree cavities but also readily accepts nest boxes. The female incubates three to seven brown and white blotched eggs for four weeks. The nestlings are ready to depart in about five weeks.

Cooper's Hawk
page 96

The Cooper's hawk is one of the attack hawks. It hides and waits for medium-sized mammals and birds, then darts out to capture them. The Cooper's hawk (fifteen to twenty inches) and the smaller sharp-shinned hawk are the most common hawks to visit bird feeders during the winter. You can recognize the Cooper's hawk by its blue-gray back.

This bird prefers a mixed habitat of trees and shrublands. It has adapted well to older suburbs with large trees. The Cooper's hawk nests high in mature trees; its four to five eggs are greenish white with spots.

Sharp-shinned Hawk
page 96

The sharp-shinned hawk is very similar in shape to the Cooper's hawk and is about ten to fourteen inches from head to tail. Like the Cooper's hawk, it has a long banded tail and ambushes its prey. Because of their similar range, habits, and coloring, these two birds are often difficult to tell apart. One distinguishing feature is the tail: the sharp-shinned hawk's tail is squared at the bottom as opposed to the rounded edge on the Cooper's hawk.

Turkey Vulture
page 96

The turkey vulture is a scavenger of dead animals. It is not often seen in yards but on roads and in nearby fields. Another name for this bird is buzzard.

The turkey vulture is a large bird, measuring from twenty-six to thirty-two inches. When walking on the ground it is similar in appearance to a black turkey, because the facial skin is red like a male turkey's wattles. Its head is red because it lacks feathers, and its legs are a dull yellow-orange. When the turkey vulture soars overhead, its six-foot wingspan points slightly upward from the body giving a V shape to the silhouette. No other soaring bird shows this configuration.

Two off-white eggs blotched with brown are laid on a cliff or in a cave. In winter the buzzard migrates to the southern states.

Canada Goose
page 96

There are about five different races of the Canada goose that live in the United States. They all have a dark gray body, white rump, black neck and head, and white chin strap that comes up behind the eye. They generally stand twenty-four to forty inches tall and can weigh up to eight or ten pounds.

The Canada goose is increasingly becoming a suburban waterfowl, especially if there is a golf course, park, or large grassy field where they can graze, as well as water nearby. Although usually considered a migratory bird (and often seen in V-formation overhead), Canada geese now overwinter in varying quantities throughout the eastern United States. They usually return to the same nesting and wintering areas each year.

A pair of Canada geese, which mate for life, makes a nest of grasses, straw, and weeds. The four to seven white eggs hatch in about twenty-eight days. Both parents take care of the young and are quite defensive.

Eastern Screech Owl
page 96

The screech owl is found throughout the eastern United States and is the most common owl in this region. If you have a number of large trees in your yard, you have the right habitat for a family of screech owls. It is a small owl, about seven to ten inches, with visible ear tufts. Two color phases, rust and gray, occur—sometimes in the same nest.

Screech owls are a welcome addition to our yards, eating lots of insects and mice. They have also been known to bathe in our birdbaths.

An owl's stomach is unique: it can digest away the nourishing food parts and leave the undigestible parts such as teeth, fur, and bones. These remains form into a small packet called a pellet, which the owl coughs up at the beginning of the day's hunting. Look for these pellets—gray oval masses of fur, feathers, teeth, and bones—at the base of trees as an indication of owl habitation.

BIRDS ON THE SIDES OF TREES

Many neighborhoods have large or mature trees used by birds for food, for protection, and for nesting. Woodpeckers and similar birds have adaptations that allow them to perch against the trunks of trees using their tail as a prop. Their bills are sharp and pointed for the purpose of prying insects from crevices in the bark.

Woodpeckers and their relatives are very beneficial birds because they eat many insects. They also provide homes for other birds and animals with the holes they excavate. Most tree-clinging birds can be attracted to yards with suet or with a mixture of peanut butter, suet, and cornmeal in equal portions.

Occasionally woodpeckers can be a nuisance, drumming on the sides of houses and even making holes in the siding. This drumming, performed to attract a mate, is usually short-lived and occurs only during breeding season. Persistent chasing of these birds can be an effective deterrent of this behavior. The excavation of holes is a more serious matter because it stems either from the presence of insects or an interest in nesting. Control of insects by insecticide is recommended. A bad-tasting spray by the name RO-PEL is also available to deter nest building and insect probing. Many state and national parks use this effectively. It is long lasting and harmless to people, pets, and wildlife.

Red-bellied Woodpecker
page 97

This brazen woodpecker is the "ruler of the roost" at a bird-feeding station. It measures between $8^1/2$ and $10^1/2$ inches. It does have a red belly, although not easily seen, consisting of a red patch at the base of the legs. A more obvious feature is the red top of its head, which extends all the way to the bill on the male, but on the female stops short, leaving a gray patch between the bill and the top of the head. In flight, the white upper rump and wing patches are quite evident.

This bird mainly eats wood-boring insects, berries, and some insects from the ground. It will also eat nuts and seeds and even store some away; it can be attracted to feeding stations with suet. It nests in tree cavities, and lay four to five white eggs in early spring.

Downy and Hairy Woodpeckers
page 97

The two most common woodpeckers in our backyards are the downy and the hairy. They are difficult to tell apart except by size. The downy is small-

**Downy and Hairy
Woodpeckers,
continued**

er (about 6^1/$_2$ to 7 inches) and more common than the hairy (7^1/$_2$ to 10 inches). Two features that distinguish these woodpeckers are the bill and outer tail feathers. The bill of the downy is small and shorter than the width of the head, whereas the hairy has a long bill, as long as the head is wide or longer. On the white outer tail feathers the downy has small black bars, but the hairy's feathers are completely white.

Both woodpeckers drum to attract a mate. They are tree cavity nesters and can easily be attracted to nest boxes. The four or five eggs are plain white. Mainly insect eaters, both woodpeckers are very beneficial. These woodpeckers also eat berries, seeds, nuts, and suet and are easily attracted to our bird-feeding stations.

Common Flicker
page 97

Also called the northern flicker, this woodpecker is frequently seen feeding on ants in our lawns. In flight the flicker exhibits extensive yellow in the wings and tail and a very conspicuous white rump patch. The male has a black patch sometimes called a mustache in a teardrop shape starting at the base of the bill. Flickers are about eleven to fourteen inches tall.

Although it is not easily attracted to a feeding station, this bird will visit a yard for the insects. Flickers perform an activity called "anting," in which they place ants in their feathers and allow them to crawl over their bodies. Little is known about why they do this; it might be of some benefit in controlling the parasites found there.

White-breasted Nuthatch
page 97

Nuthatches, sometimes nicknamed "upside-down birds," are the only birds that consistently feed head downward on a tree trunk. The white-breasted nuthatch is approximately five to six inches high; its coloring is blue-grey with a white underside. In the male the top of the head is black from the bill to the shoulder; the

White-breasted Nuthatch, continued

female has a black cap but a dark gray color over most of the head returning to black at the shoulder.

The white-breasted nuthatch can be found in any neighborhood that has trees. It comes readily to bird feeders, eating sunflower and suet. Because it is unable to crush sunflower seeds in its delicate beak, the nuthatch takes the seeds to a nearby tree, stashes them in a small crevice, and then proceeds to pick them open to remove the hearts.

The white-breasted nuthatch nests in tree cavities and lays five to eight white eggs. White-breasted nuthatches can be attracted to nest boxes readily, especially boxes placed high in a tree. They eat many insects and are very beneficial birds.

Red-breasted Nuthatch
page 97

Not as common as the white-breasted nuthatch, this smaller version ($4^1/2$ to 5 inches) nests only in the higher elevations and extreme northern states. In the fall and winter months it can be quite common throughout the United States. It has the same basic coloration as that of the white-breasted nuthatch except that the sides are buff instead of white. The female has a dark gray cap and the male has the characteristic black cap.

The red-breasted nuthatch prefers coniferous trees. The five to six white eggs, spotted with reddish brown, are laid in a tree cavity.

Brown Creeper
page 97

The brown creeper is a definite bonus to anyone who feeds suet. This small, quiet bird is easily overlooked as it spirals up a tree looking like a piece of bark. It is small, five to six inches, with a down-curved, slender bill. A northern resident in the summer, it can be found throughout the eastern United States during the winter. The brown creeper has a stiff tail and uses it to prop itself against tree trunks. These birds build nests on the sides of trees or on rotted limbs and occasionally in the nest cavities of woodpeckers. The five to six eggs are white with brown spots.

PERCHING BIRDS

Perching birds are the largest group of birds in the world. Many of the birds that we see in our neighborhoods belong to this group. They are attractive and normally quite visible. They have pleasant songs that they use to attract mates and to defend territories during the breeding season. Calls different from their songs may be used to indicate danger and to locate each other.

The perching birds are named for their ability to perch on small twigs and wires. Their normal toe arrangement—three toes forward and one backward, all originating from the same location—gives them the ability to grip. The muscles and tendons in the feet and legs do not relax as ours do when we sleep, thus the bird can sleep while perching. If the bird tips off balance the toes tighten up automatically.

Because these birds are numerous and usually quite colorful, this section divides the birds by color. A few birds will appear in more than one division because of their color variations, so try various sections if you have trouble finding the bird you're looking for. If you can't find it at all, the bird might be a rare species in your area.

• • • • • • • RED BIRDS • • • • • • • •

Although we may think of red birds as being quite visible and easily seen, in actuality they can hide themselves quite well in the vegetation. Most red birds are either tree dwelling or shrub dwelling, such as the scarlet tanager that lives in the tops of trees. Most of the red birds, at least the brightly colored red ones, are males. The females are either brown, gray, or olive green.

Northern Cardinal
page 98

One of our most colorful birds, the cardinal can be found in shrubs as well as in small trees. The male and female both have crests and red bills, but the female is a creamy brown with reddish colors on her back, wings, and tail. The cardinal's bill is heavy because it is used for cracking seeds such as sunflower. This bird typically measures eight to nine inches.

Cardinals like to nest in thick, heavy shrubs. The nest is constructed of loosely arranged twigs, weed stalks, bark, and grasses and lined with fine grasses and hair. They usually lay three to five gray-white eggs with purple and brown markings and may nest more than once in a season. They hatch in eleven to twelve days and fledge ten days later. This is a common bird at your sunflower feeder.

Purple Finch
page 98

This raspberry-colored member of the sparrow family is most common at feeders during winter. The male's red back distinguishes him from the brown-backed male house finch. The female is striped brown. Both male and female have deeply notched tails and are five to six inches high.

This bird nests in the northern states in conifer trees on a horizontal branch. The nest is made of twigs and grasses and lined with fine grasses and hair. Three to five pale greenish blue eggs are usually laid. They hatch in two weeks and the young leave the nest two weeks later. The purple finch is common at both thistle and sunflower seed feeders.

House Finch
page 98

In the early 1940s, house finches were brought as caged pet birds from the West to the New York area. Enough escaped, over time, to establish it as a wild bird. The numbers of house finches have increased, and in many areas it is one of the most common birds seen at feeders, both thistle and sunflower. The male can be anywhere from red to orange to almost yellow (see yellow birds). Its brown back has no red coloring. The female is dull gray with heavy striping. This finch measures about $5^{1}/_{2}$ inches.

House finches' nests usually contain three to five pale greenish blue eggs with brown markings and can be found in nest boxes, on ledges, or in cavities around buildings. The chicks hatch in two weeks but may take up to twenty days to fledge.

Scarlet Tanager
page 98

A bird that frequents mature trees, the scarlet tanager male is bright red with black wings and tail; the female is dull green above with yellow-green under-

Scarlet Tanager,
continued

parts and dark gray wings and tail (see yellow birds). Both birds are approximately seven inches.

The scarlet tanager can be found from the southern Ohio valley northward. During the early part of spring, this beautiful bird feeds quite close to the ground. Its nest, built of loosely placed twigs, weeds, and grasses, protects the three to five blue-green eggs marked with brown. The incubation period is two weeks and the young depart after ten days. An insect eater not attracted to birdseed, the scarlet tanager can be enticed with a running-water birdbath.

Summer Tanager
page 98

The male summer tanager is scarlet red all over, even most of his wings. The female is an almost uniform yellow-green, perhaps a little darker on her upper body (see yellow birds). It is a bit larger than the scarlet tanager at $7^1/2$ inches.

The summer tanager is abundant in the southern oaks and suburbs from the Ohio valley southward. It eats insects but can be attracted to a birdbath. Three to four blue-green eggs marked with brown are laid in a nest woven of weeds, leaves, grasses, and bark. It takes twelve days to hatch the eggs and another two weeks for the young birds to fledge.

Ruby-throated Hummingbird
page 98

The ruby-throat is the most common hummingbird found in the eastern United States. It is also our smallest bird, measuring only $3^1/2$ inches. The male can be identified by his bright iridescent red throat, white belly, and iridescent green back and head. The female looks similar but lacks the red throat (see greenish brown birds).

Ruby-throats like to nest near water. The nest, composed of thistle down, spider webs, and lichens, is about $1^1/2$ inches across and is built entirely by the female, perhaps because the flashy male would attract predators to the area. Two white eggs are laid and the female alone raises the young. It takes

Ruby-throated Hummingbird, continued

two weeks for her to incubate the eggs and from two to four weeks (depending on the food supply) for the young to leave.

Hummingbirds are one of the most beautiful and enjoyable birds you can attract to your yard by feeders and plantings. They are drawn to red and orange long-tubed flowers such as columbine and fuchsia. These tiny gems can also be enticed with a nectar feeder. Use a red-colored feeder with a sugar solution of one part sugar to four parts water. Ruby-throats remember from year to year the location of flowers and feeders, so once you have them sipping your nectar, you will have years of enjoyment to come.

• • • • • • • YELLOW BIRDS • • • • • • •

Although yellow birds may seem to be quite visible, they can hide very easily among the green leaves in a summer's light. The yellow birds we see in our yards are most often small and appear only during the spring, summer, and early fall.

Yellow Warbler
page 99

The yellow warbler is yellow all over, though the male does have some reddish brown streaking on the breast that some liken to dripped tobacco juice. These stripes are absent on the female or are very faint. It measures between $4^1/2$ and $5^1/2$ inches. Normally a bird of the wetlands, the yellow warbler has also adapted to the shrubs of our backyards.

The female builds the nest by herself for the most part, then lays four to five light green or blue eggs spotted around the end with brown. They are incubated for ten to twelve days. The young are able to leave after another ten to twelve days. The yellow warbler begins migrating south in late summer.

Yellow-rumped Warbler
page 99

The yellow-rumped warbler is about six inches long and is easily recognized by its bright yellow upper rump. Yellow patches also appear on the shoulders and the top of the head, especially in the males. The fall warbler and the female are drab except for these yellow spots. During the breeding season the male has a black face and white throat.

The yellow-rump has a habit of flicking its tail when hopping through the trees. It winters from the Great Lakes south and nests predominantly in the northern United States and southern Canada. This is one of the first warblers to migrate in the spring and the last to leave in the fall.

Three to five creamy white eggs marked with brown are laid in a nest of bark, small twigs, leaves, and weeds. Plant fibers and feathers are often placed loosely in the nest to conceal the eggs when the parents are absent. It takes about twelve days for the eggs to hatch and another twelve to fourteen days for the young birds to fledge.

The yellow-rumped warbler used to be called the myrtle warbler, because in winter it is fond of poison ivy berries and myrtle berries. During summer the yellow-rumps flit about eating insects from the air, especially near waterways, much as flycatchers do.

Magnolia Warbler
page 99

Although it breeds only in the northern part of the United States, the magnolia warbler visits our yards in good numbers during migration. The yellow breast of the male has black broken streaks; the streaks on the breast of the female are less prominent. The magnolia warbler is the same size as the yellow warbler: $4^1/2$ to $5^1/2$ inches. Four to five greenish white eggs, spotted with brown, are laid in May or June and hatch in eleven to fourteen days. The young leave the nest in another ten days.

Evening Grosbeak
page 99

When this big "goldfinch" (7 to $8^1/2$ inches) shows up at our sunflower feeders, it causes quite a stir. Usually twenty to fifty grosbeaks move around together descending on one neighborhood after another and eating prodigious amounts of sunflower seed. Both males and females have large bills; the

Evening Grosbeak, continued

male's is yellow and the female's a gray-green. The female's body is a light gray (see gray birds).

Three to four pale blue eggs are laid that hatch in about two weeks. The young leave two weeks later. The evening grosbeak nests in the extreme northern United States and Canada but makes its presence known during winter when it invades the feeders throughout the northern half of the eastern United States.

American Goldfinch
page 99

There is probably no suburban bird as popular as the goldfinch, or wild canary as many call it. During the breeding season the male goldfinch is an extremely bright yellow. Both male and female have black wings and tail; the male also has a black cap. During the winter the male goldfinch molts to an olive yellow color, losing his black cap. This molt makes the sexes indistinguishable. Wing bars are white during the summer and change to buff during the winter. In flight, the white rump or upper tail is prominent. This bird measures between $4^1/2$ and $5^1/2$ inches.

Goldfinches are late nesters, raising their families in July and August. Their nest is made from the down of thistle, willow, milkweed, and other finely textured plants. The nest is so tightly woven it will hold water, sometimes drowning the baby birds during hard rains. Four to five light blue eggs are laid and incubated by the female.

Primarily seed eaters, goldfinches are wonderful birds to bring to your backyard with a feeding station. Readily attracted to sunflower and niger, they are perky, happy birds to have around. Buying a feeder for niger and putting it out with niger seed will almost always attract goldfinches within three weeks. Many report success within hours. Goldfinches shift ranges, so they are often absent from feeders in late spring and early fall.

Scarlet Tanager, Female
page 99

The female scarlet tanager is not bright red as is the male (see red birds). She has dark gray on her wings similar to the black on the male, but is a greenish yellow where the male is red. In the fall, males and young birds resemble the female.

Summer Tanager, Female

The female summer tanager is a yellowish green. The lower body is a brighter yellow or yellowish green than the darker, olive green upper body. The summer tanager does not have the darker wings of the female scarlet tanager, but overall the two look very similar. The scarlet and summer tanagers can usually be distinguished from warblers by their size and by their darker head and cheek patch. The female, like the red male (see red birds), is 7 to 7 1/2 inches long.

House Finch
page 99

About ten to twenty percent of the male house finches seen are of the yellow or orange race. The house finch may soon be our most common bird at a feeding station, readily feeding on niger and sunflower. The house finch is discussed in detail in the red bird section.

• • • • • • • ORANGE BIRDS • • • • • • • •

Orange birds in our neighborhoods are quite striking, but sometimes amazingly overlooked. Once the leaves are back on the trees, they blend in quite well.

Northern or Baltimore Oriole
page 100

Formerly known as the Baltimore oriole, the northern oriole is one of the few insect-eating birds we can easily attract to our yards. The male oriole is bright orange with a black head, and the female has an orange-yellow body with a gray head. Both male and female are seven to eight inches high.

The oriole's nest, a hanging pouch that the birds enter from the top, is made of woven strings, hair, and plant fibers and lined with hair, grasses, and down. Four to six gray to pale blue-white eggs with some streaking or blotching are laid. After two weeks the eggs hatch; the young birds leave the nest in another two weeks.

Northern orioles are insect and berry eaters and cannot be attracted to seed feeders. When returning from the southern coasts of the United States and the tropics in the spring, orioles can be attracted to nectar, jelly, and fruit feeders. The best way to initially attract the oriole is to place cut orange halves on feeders. Once they begin coming to the oranges, they can be converted to a nectar or jelly feeder.

American Robin

page 100

This bird of the thrush family is easily recognized by its brick orange breast. Normally a woodland thrush, the robin has adapted well to suburban life. One of the larger perching birds, it measures between nine and eleven inches.

A berry and insect eater, the robin will feed on insects and earthworms in our lawns during the summer. It also eats the berries from our native plants and from ornamental shrubs and trees. Although a number of robins overwinter in the north, they are usually touted as an indicator of spring, arriving early with their cheery song.

Occasionally a late spring snowstorm will cause concern for these early migrants. Since they do not eat birdseed, they can be under significant stress. Clearing snow from a spot and putting out raisins, chopped fruit, or moistened dog food can help them through this difficult time.

Robins normally nest on large limbs or branches but have adapted to most any flat surface. Windowsills, fences, lamp posts, porch pillars, gables, and eaves are favorite places. The nest is usually built out of reach of direct rainfall. Nests are made first of grass and other flexible plant materials, then lined with mud, making a deep bowl. The mud bowl is then lined with finer grass. Four to five blue eggs are laid; they hatch in two weeks and the young leave in about fourteen to sixteen days. Two to three nestings occur each year. The young have a much paler orange spotted breast and sometimes light streaks or spots on their backs.

American Redstart
page 100

This warbler is easily identified because no other warbler or small bird is black and orange with a white belly. There is bright orange on the shoulder and large, very patchy orange spots on the tail. The female replaces the orange with yellow, and the white is more extensive on the underside up to her throat. Additionally, the black is grayer on the female. This bird has the habit of fanning its tail upon landing, weaving it back and forth, slowly putting the feathers back. The redstart is the same size as other warblers, $4^1/2$ to $5^1/2$ inches.

Found quite extensively in the eastern United States, it is most often seen in early migration. This perky little bird likes the forests and can be found in older neighborhoods with large trees and mature shrubs. The nest built of bark, grasses, lichens, and other plant fibers holds four to five creamy white eggs speckled with brown. The eggs hatch in twelve to fourteen days and the young mature rapidly, leaving the nest in nine to ten days.

Rufous-sided Towhee
page 100

A welcome sign of spring in the north, the rufous-sided towhee is a strikingly attractive bird. Its sides are a rust orange and the belly is white. The male has black on its throat, tail, head, and chest; the female is dark brown where the male is black. The eyes of both sexes are a pretty red. They measure between 7 and $8^1/2$ inches.

The towhee nests in the northern United States but is common throughout the states during migration. It winters over most of the United States except in the far north. The towhee searches for insects and seeds on the ground near and under our feeders. During the winter, scattering raisins or berries will keep them coming to your yard.

The rufous-sided towhee nests in shrubs, vines, and thickets. Its nest is made of grass, bark, twigs, and leaves. Four to five spotted off-white to green-white eggs hatch in two weeks. The young fledge in ten to twelve days.

• • • • • • • **GRAY BIRDS** • • • • • • •

Working as a naturalist, one of the hardest jobs I had was identifying a bird over the phone. Most often it was a gray bird with no special characteristics. Since female birds are usually the primary incubators, they are less brightly colored than the showy males, hence they are gray birds with no distinguishing markings. However, even the drabbest bird has some identifying features, including accompanying immature birds and fully colored males, so identification is usually possible.

Mockingbird
page 101

The mockingbird is probably the best known suburban bird in the southern United States that does not readily come to a birdseed feeder. Noted for its extremely variable calls, the mockingbird can mimic almost any sound. It has been known to mimic over one hundred different bird calls as well as man-made noises. One good mimic was even able to imitate a school bell, thereby dismissing classes.

The mockingbird is a large perching bird, about nine to eleven inches. It nests in shrubs, trees, and vines. The nest is made of twigs lined with numerous kinds of soft plant material, or even string, yarn, wool, and paper. Four to five blue-green eggs spotted with brown are laid and hatch in about twelve days. The northern range of the mockingbird is determined by the availability of winter berries and the severity of the winters. Suet and berries can be used to attract mockingbirds to your yard as well as natural plantings of shrubs and trees that produce fruit. A bird bath is also a welcome sight to these birds.

Gray Catbird
page 101

Another bird that mimics others, the gray catbird, has adapted well to the suburban way of life and

**Gray Catbird,
continued**

lives in the trees and shrubs of our yards. Although it can imitate well, the gray catbird has its own set of calls. The catbird gets its name because of the catlike "mew" it gives, especially during the morning and evening hours. It is nine inches in length.

The nest of the catbird is usually in a dense shrub such as a lilac or mock orange. When I was growing up, we had a catbird nest in the mock orange outside our bedroom window every year. The nest is constructed of small sticks, weed stems, bark shreds, leaves, grasses, hair, and even string. The inner nest is lined with hair, fine grasses, and pine needles. The eggs, usually five in number, are a dark blue-green. They hatch in two weeks, and it takes another two weeks for the young to leave.

Carolina Chickadee and Black-capped Chickadee
page 101

The most amicable and fun-to-watch bird we can attract to our backyards is the chickadee. Either the black-capped chickadee or Carolina chickadee is found throughout the eastern United States. Their habitats are similar. The Carolina is a more southern bird whereas the black-capped chickadee is more northern. The two overlap in their ranges in a band about halfway up the United States, meeting in Indiana, Illinois, Ohio, and Pennsylvania. Both birds are between $4^1/2$ and 5 inches.

Chickadees come readily to bird feeders. They especially like sunflower. They take the seed to a nearby perch, put it between their toes, and peck it open for the nut meat.

The chickadee nests in tree cavities and will readily come to a nest box. Use a nest box with a $1^1/8$-inch hole to deter house sparrows. It lines its nest with plant and animal materials such as mosses, wool, and hair. The chickadee lays five to seven or more white eggs with brown specks. The chicks hatch in about two weeks and leave the nest in sixteen days or longer depending on the size of the brood. These perky little birds can become quite tame, even eating seed from your hand.

Dark-eyed Junco
page 101

The junco, or snowbird as many call him, is a true indication that winter is on the way. It is a bird that normally breeds in Canada and in the coniferous forests of the northern United States and the Appalachians. It can be found throughout the eastern United States during winter. It is easily distinguished from other gray birds by the two white outer tail feathers. In size it measures $5^{1}/_{2}$ to $6^{1}/_{2}$ inches.

The junco is a ground bird at feeders during the winter, rarely feeding at a bin feeder or a tube feeder. Millet is its preferred food. Very territorial when feeding, the junco will not let another junco approach any nearer than about eight inches. If one dares to get closer, the junco flashes its two white outer tail feathers and chases it off. It commonly feeds in flocks, and the call notes exchanged between the juncos and tree sparrows sound like little bells in the weeds. This is a pleasant bird to have around.

Tufted Titmouse
page 101

The tufted titmouse is an easily identified bird because it is the only small bird with a crest. The large black eye gives it a mouselike appearance. It is fond of woodlots and well wooded yards. It measures about 6 to $6^{1}/_{2}$ inches.

The tufted titmouse is a common visitor to suburban neighborhoods. At feeders it has a definite preference for sunflower seeds, taking them one at a time to a nearby perch and pecking them open. A cavity nester, the tufted titmouse can sometimes be persuaded to lay its five to six white speckled eggs in a birdhouse. The young hatch in two weeks and leave the nest about two and a half weeks later.

Chimney Swift
page 101

The chimney swift is most often seen flying above our cities and yards. Around homes it uses chimneys for nesting instead of traditional hollow trees or caves.

With the sky as a background, the chimney swift will appear to be black, however it is actually a gray-

Chimney Swift, continued

ish brown. Look for a short (about 5^1/$_2$ inches) "stogy" with wings, twittering and alternating fast wing beats with gliding. The chimney swift catches many insects.

Five white eggs are laid in a shallow cup of twigs glued to the insides of a chimney with the swift's saliva. It takes three weeks for the young to hatch and another four weeks or more for them to leave the nest.

Rock Dove

The rock dove, or pigeon as most of us know it, is truly a domestic bird. It is one of the larger perching birds, about twelve to fourteen inches. Nesting comfortably on building ledges or any small platform, the rock dove can have numerous clutches every year during the warm months. The nest is usually made of a few sticks to keep the two white eggs from rolling. The eggs take nineteen days to hatch and the young leave in about five weeks. Hybrids make for bizarre color variations from white to red to all sorts of speckles.

Rock doves can become a nuisance in cities and at bird feeders. Providing feeders that the rock dove cannot land on works well. Eliminating nesting sites helps in population control.

Common Nighthawk
page 101

Nighthawks, as their name implies, are frequently seen at night above suburban yards or around street lights catching insects on the wing. If we see them during the daytime they are normally sitting on a tree stump, horizontal limb, rooftop, or other flat surface. They are actually not hawks but belong to the goatsucker family, which are insect eaters.

The common nighthawk is a gray-brown bird with very narrow but long pointed wings with a wing spread of about two feet. It is rather small, about eight to ten inches high. Its wing feathers are a mottled, dark gray with two very prominent white patches near the end of the wings and a white patch on the throat. It has a flat head and a huge mouth opening, although its bill is small. The nighthawk uses its large gaping mouth to scoop up insects as it flies through the air.

The nest is usually on a flat area on the ground or on a flat rooftop. Two cream-colored eggs with grayish brown blotches are laid and hatch in three weeks. The young depart in another three weeks. The nighthawk, a very beneficial bird, is also called the mosquito hawk because it eats thousands of insects nightly.

• • • • • • • **BLUE BIRDS** • • • • • • •

There are a number of birds in our yards that are colored blue or at least appear to be blue. Some of them are bright like the blue jay, while others are slate blue or very dark blue. Sometimes the blue is only noticeable when light hits the bird a certain way, such as in the purple martins and tree swallows.

Blue Jay
page 102

The blue jay, a large bird at 11 to $12^1/2$ inches, is one of the birds with a crest. It will sometimes imitate other birds' calls. The blue jay is fond of bird feeders, especially those containing sunflower and suet.

Blue jays usually nest in a tree; the foundation of the nest is broken twigs and the lining is made of grasses, yarn, and dead plant material. It is fun to put different colored yarn in the yard and watch to see where it is taken by the blue jays. Four or five pale green eggs with brown spots are laid. It takes around two and a half weeks for the eggs to hatch and another three weeks before the young are ready to leave.

Blue jays are interesting birds to have at your bird feeders because of their intelligent behavior. They have been observed opening containers to reach the seed and opening peanut shells for the peanuts. They are sometimes considered nuisances because they tend to dominate feeders and keep the smaller birds away. A number of companies have introduced what they call blue jay-repelling or blue

**Blue Jay,
continued**

jay-proof feeders that allow only the smaller birds to feed.

Since the jays are present all year long, many people do not realize that they migrate. Good numbers of them will start migration during the early fall in September and October. The northern birds move south, and the far north then has a lack of blue jays for the wintertime. As spring approaches the birds migrate northward again.

Indigo Bunting
page 102

The indigo bunting is a small bird (approximately 5^1/$_2$ inches) that is found at the edges of forests and meadows as well as in our yards. It is a very deep blue, sometimes even appearing black. The bill is a light gray or light blue. The female is brown (her description appears in the brown section).

The female nests close to the ground in shrubs or in a raspberry or bramble thicket. Four or five blue-white eggs are laid in a deep cup made of dried grasses, pieces of dead leaves, bits of snakeskin, bark, and twigs. The sides of the cup have linings of wool, fine grasses, and even cattle and horse hair. The female incubates the eggs about two weeks. After another ten days of rearing, the young are able to live on their own.

The indigo bunting is basically an insect eater. In the springtime, however, during early migration, it can be attracted to thistle at our bird feeding stations.

Eastern Bluebird
page 102

No bird has caused such a stir as the eastern bluebird. More and more people are trying to attract these birds and provide them with suitable nesting habitat. The female is not as bright a blue as the male, sometimes approaching brown, but still has the same orange and white underside. Both male and female measure from 6^1/$_2$ to 7^1/$_2$ inches.

Bluebirds were common in the early part of the century. But because they are cavity nesters the bluebirds have had a difficult time due to the loss of nesting habitat. They like forest edges, old orchards, and old meadows. They prefer habitat that provides high perches where they can sit and watch for insects on the ground.

Although these birds are somewhat migratory, most of the United States does keep bluebirds during the wintertime. This is when feeders can be very important to them. The feeders are also helpful in the springtime when early snows may catch returning birds unprepared. They are fond of berries and can be attracted to a feeder if berries and insects are used. They also will use a birdbath readily.

Many states now have bluebird societies that perpetuate the placing of nest boxes and the restoring of habitat for bluebirds. Thanks to such societies and to concerned citizens the bluebird is making a comeback in the eastern United States.

Purple Martin
page 102

The purple martin is our largest swallow, measuring between 7 1/2 and 8 1/2 inches. Unlike other swallows, the male and female are colored differently. The male purple martin is a blue-black all over—it is the only bird in the swallow family to have a black front. The female is gray-blue with gray-white undersides. Both exhibit a bit of a forked tail. The purple martin arrives in the United States from South America in the last part of January, making its way to the northern parts as late as the first of April.

Interest in providing the purple martins with places to nest is growing. In the past the purple martin nested in hollow trees. Today most martins nest in colonies using man-made structures. Martins make their nests out of leaves, feathers, grasses, twigs, small pieces of bark, and other plant fiber. About five white eggs are laid. It takes fifteen to sixteen days for the eggs to hatch. In another four weeks the young will leave the nest. Purple martins have only one brood of young per year. Keeping martin houses available to the birds all summer

**Purple Martin,
continued**

allows the new males an opportunity to locate a place to nest for the following year.

An important habitat consideration in placing a martin house is its close proximity to water. The birds use this water expanse as a feeding ground, eating the many insects that frequent wet areas. Another important habitat need is an open area around the house of at least fifty feet and preferably more because the birds make a gliding entrance to their homes.

Feeding primarily on the wing, the purple martin eats many flying insects. It has been said that it eats as many as ten thousand mosquitoes per day. But much of the time the purple martin eats larger insects and those that fly high. The martins also drink on the wing, skimming over the water.

Barn Swallow
page 102

The barn swallow is the only swallow with a true forked tail. It is deeply forked and has white spots. Barn swallows are 6 to 7 $1/2$ inches in size.

The barn swallow is a common bird in many suburban areas, nesting inside garages, barns, porches, and on the tops of beams. It feeds on the wing catching flying insects, and probably does more for mosquito control in a yard than does the purple martin. Barn swallows make their mud nests by picking up little clay pellets near rain puddles along driveways and fields. The nests are lined with different kinds of grasses, straw, white poultry feathers, hair, and bits of leaves. Usually five white eggs with brown spots are laid. It takes about two and a half weeks for the young to hatch and three more weeks for them to leave the nest. Once these sociable, pretty birds are successful at nesting in a spot, they will return year after year. Many times they bring a flock in migration with them, so you may be inundated with ten to forty barn swallows looking over a nesting site.

Tree Swallow
page 103

The tree swallow is a cavity nester, often using blue-bird houses and martin houses. It has an iridescent green or an iridescent blue sheen depending on the light. It is the only swallow that has white on its underside. The tail is not nearly as forked as the purple martin's. This bird is a bit smaller than the barn swallow at five to six inches.

Readily making use of woodpecker holes in trees, the tree swallow also loves to nest in bluebird boxes as they apparently are the correct size. They some-times compete with the bluebirds for these homes. The nest cavity is lined with grasses, straw, leaves, and even white chicken feathers. These feathers seem to be a trademark of the tree swallow. Four to six white eggs are laid taking about sixteen days to hatch. The young leave in about three weeks. Once they have a successful nesting in a certain location, tree swallows will return year after year.

The tree swallow is the earliest swallow to return in spring migration. It feeds mainly on insects while flying. If it is early in the season and insects are not available, it will feed on seeds and berries. Along with the barn swallow, the tree swallow is probably one of the most competent birds at controlling insects around the yard. It flies back and forth catching mosquitoes, gnats, and black flies as well as larger insects.

• • • • • GREENISH BROWN BIRDS • • • • •

The greenish brown birds are basically a nondescript group, neither brown nor gray but having an olive color or tint to their feathers. Most of these birds fre-quent bushes and trees.

Red-eyed Vireo
page 103

The red-eyed vireo is probably the most numerous bird in the eastern deciduous forest, although there are some indications that it is declining in popula-tion. This is possibly due to the destruction of forests. It nests in older communities where there are larger trees. The red-eyed vireo feeds mainly in

Red-eyed Vireo,
continued

the tops of trees, eating many insects and caterpillars, and is an effective enemy of the gypsy moth. It stands at about six inches.

This vireo sings most of the day and often into the night. It also sings while feeding and sitting on the nest. The nest is usually built in a small fork of a tree limb, hanging near the end of the branch, or in a tall shrub. It is made with intricately woven plant materials including fine grasses, bits of bark, and grapevine paper and is fastened together with spider and tent caterpillar silk. Four eggs are laid. These are white with a few black and brown spots. It takes about two weeks for the eggs to hatch and another two weeks for the young to leave the nest. During this time, the parents feed the young almost constantly during the daylight hours.

Warbling Vireo
page 103

The warbling vireo has the lightest coloration of all the vireos. It is a light gray-green with an underside of light gray; occasionally you will see a buff color along the sides. At five to six inches, it is a bit smaller than the red-eyed vireo.

The warbling vireo's nest is similar to that of other vireos. It is a cup suspended from the end of a branch, woven out of grasses, other plant materials, and hair. It also uses spider webs and lichens to decorate the outside and hold it together. Four or five white eggs, very sparsely spotted with browns and blacks, make up the clutch. It takes about fourteen days for the eggs to hatch and another two weeks for the young to leave.

Eastern Phoebe

The eastern phoebe is one of the flycatchers. It is distinguished from other flycatchers by the absence of wing bars and measures between 6 1/2 and 7 inches. It has a habit of bobbing its tail, especially when it is at rest. The eastern phoebe is a welcome bird in any neighborhood because it feeds on insects.

**Eastern Phoebe,
continued**

The nest is usually built on a flat structure such as a shelf. It is often found around bridges but can also be near homes. Many people put out phoebe shelves similar to robin shelves to attract this bird. The nest is made out of weeds, sticks, and grasses and lined with hair and sheep wool as well as cocoons and silk from spider webs. Four or five white eggs are laid. Occasionally they will have brown spots on them. After fourteen days the eggs hatch, and the nestlings depart in another fourteen days or so. It is one of our very early migrant birds and comes back to the same spot year after year.

Willow Flycatcher
page 103

The willow flycatcher may be seen in neighborhood shrubs. It is smaller than the phoebe (about 5 1/2 to 6 inches) and the lower part of the bill is yellow whereas in the phoebe it is all black.

The nest is usually found in willows, rosebushes, or shrubs in our yards. It is built about eight or ten feet above the ground. It is made of shredded bark, grasses, plant stems, and any kind of cotton material that can be found. Four eggs are usually laid. These are buff in color with spots near one end. It takes two weeks to incubate the eggs and another two weeks before the young are large enough to fledge. Flycatchers are good birds to have around because they catch many insects. The willow flycatcher sits on a branch, darts out to capture insects, and comes back to its perch again.

**Ruby-throated
Hummingbird,
Female**
page 103

The ruby-throated hummingbird is covered in the red bird section but is also discussed here because the female has a greenish back. She also has a white belly and a small white spot behind the eye. The female hummingbird is easy to identify by its tiny size (3 1/2 inches). It also has a very long bill and is the only bird that truly hovers. It usually frequents flowers. The immature male looks similar to the female. Look under red birds for more information about the ruby-throat.

Tree Swallow
page 103

The tree swallow is covered in the blue section and is only mentioned here because it may also appear iridescent green depending on how the light strikes it. The immature tree swallow can be a brownish green on its upper parts.

• • • • • • • • **BROWN BIRDS** • • • • • • • •

Many birds are called "little brown jobs" by those who attempt to identify them. These birds can sometimes be very difficult to name, but if one takes time, taking into account their size, bill shape, body shape, habitat, and the way they feed, most can be identified. The females of many species are brown, so watch carefully to see which males accompany them.

House Wren
page 104

Next to the robin, the house wren is probably the easiest bird to attract to a nest box. The wren is a gray-brown bird with darker brown on the back and lighter brown on the belly. It characteristically holds its tail erect as do most of the wrens.

The small house wren (4 $1/2$ to 5 inches) is easily attracted to a nest box, which should have an opening of 1 $1/8$ inches to prevent larger birds from using it. The box size itself may vary. This wren, however, will use almost any cavity to build its nest in, from teakettles to bumpers to tin cans. The nest is made entirely of sticks of different sizes with the small ones on top. The male will fill numerous nesting sites with sticks to attract the female. The female eventually chooses one but will rearrange it many times, or even take it completely apart and put it back together again.

The house wren is very territorial. Unless you have a large yard, you may have only one pair nesting there. House wrens will often kill other birds including other wrens found in their territory, especially when they are raising young. Anywhere from five to

**House Wren,
continued**

eleven eggs are laid that hatch in about two weeks. The young leave the nest in twelve to nineteen days depending on the size of the brood and the food supply in the area. Two to three broods can be raised in one season, so a yard may be inundated with young wrens at different times of the year.

The house wren is a desirable bird to have in your yard, not only because of its perkiness and exquisite call but, being a voracious insect eater, it may do a lot of damage to the insect populations. Everyone loves to have the "jenny wren" in their yard.

Bewick's Wren
page 104

The Bewick's wren is a little larger than the house wren (5 to 5 1/2 inches) and has more striking characteristics. It has a definite white eye stripe above the eye and a black stripe through the eye. The tail is significantly longer than that of other wrens and has white tail spots.

The Bewick's wren is becoming less numerous, basically nesting in the central part of eastern North America and wintering in the southern part. It can be found in the shrubs around your yard or feeding on insects on the ground.

Like the house wren, the Bewick's wren nests in tree cavities or in any type of cavity it can find. It will use sticks to build its nest, but it will also use other types of plant material such as leaves, grasses, hair, pieces of wool, and cast-off snakeskins. Frequently it will use feathers. Four to five white eggs make up the clutch. These are sometimes spotted with numerous different colors ranging from brown to purple to gray. As with the house wren, it takes fourteen days for the eggs to hatch and another two weeks for the birds to leave.

Carolina Wren
page 104

The Carolina wren is our largest eastern wren, measuring 5 1/2 to 6 inches. It has striking characteristics, including a very pronounced white eye stripe above the eye. It likes to live in areas with mature

Carolina Wren,
continued

trees and many shrubs, feeding in the bushes and on the ground.

The Carolina wren is not quite as specific in its nesting habits as the other wrens. It will use nest boxes but will also use places that have an open roof such as tree stumps, crotches of trees, flower baskets, or any cavity where it can make itself hidden. The nest is made out of grasses, weed pieces, leaves, bark, and roots and then lined with smaller pieces of hair, snakeskin, and feathers. Five to six white eggs, sometimes speckled, are laid. The female incubates for about two weeks, then in two more weeks her brood is gone.

Brown Thrasher
page 104

The brown thrasher can hardly be considered a "little brown job." It is a very large bird, $10^1/2$ to 12 inches, with a rusty, reddish brown upper body and a down-curved, pointed bill. Being a larger bird, it eats much bigger prey such as small frogs and snails. It feeds on the ground, catching many insects that may damage our backyard plants.

The brown thrasher is one of the many thrushes or mimic birds that can imitate other birds. Although it normally sings from a high bush or a tree, the brown thrasher nests in shrubs. It constructs a nest from layers of different plant materials, such as dead leaves, twigs, bark, grasses, and tiny parts of roots. These layers eventually turn into a nice cup at the top. The female lays four to six white eggs with a pale blue cast. These can be spotted with brown. It takes about two weeks for the birds to hatch the eggs with both male and female tending the nest. Another two weeks or more elapse before the fledglings leave. Two nestings can occur during one year.

Wood Thrush
page 104

The wood thrush, like the robin, is in the thrush family, though at $7^1/2$ to $8^1/2$ inches it is smaller than the robin. In the eastern United States it is the most

**Wood Thrush,
continued**

common thrush in suburban yards with mature deciduous trees. It is easily recognized because it likes to scratch in the leaves on the ground where it catches many insects.

The wood thrush likes to nest on a branch or in the crotch of a tree. The nest is similar to the robin's except it does not contain as much mud. The thrush uses plant materials that are commonly found in the forest, such as leaves, tiny pieces of twigs, and roots. Characteristic of most of the thrushes, the wood thrush lays four blue or blue-green eggs in its nest. The female incubates the eggs for about two weeks before they hatch. Two weeks later the young emerge fully feathered and fly away. Two broods of young can be reared each year.

Cedar Waxwing
page 104

The cedar waxwing is a common backyard bird wherever we have berries. It is easily recognized by its tuft, or crest, which is much like that of a blue jay or a cardinal. The cedar waxwing is an elegant light brown bird larger than a sparrow (seven to eight inches). The secondary wing feather tips exude a bright red waxy substance.

The cedar waxwing primarily eats berries and insects. When berries are not plentiful this bird is usually absent, but when they are you may see up to a few hundred cedar waxwings in one area. They are called vagrant migrants because they follow the berry crops and are not in any area at a specific time. You can see cedar waxwings in the summer along stream and river banks. They will commonly sit on a branch from which they dive out across the water to catch insects as they emerge from the water.

Their nests are found in either deciduous or coniferous trees. The nest is built of small sticks, dried grasses, weed stalks, mosses, pine needles, and whatever other dead material can be found. The inside of the nest is lined with wool and hair. Often cedar waxwings can be found around the yard pick-

**Cedar Waxwing,
continued**

ing up pieces of string, yarn, and wool. The typical clutch is five pale gray to blue eggs speckled with black. It takes fifteen to sixteen days for them to hatch and fourteen to eighteen days for the young to leave the nest. If your backyard has a good supply of berries, more than likely you can entice these birds back every year. Some people have been successful in attracting these birds to a feeder offering berries, chopped apples, raisins, and dried currants.

Brown-headed Cowbird
page 105

The brown-headed cowbird is an easily recognized bird. The male is a black-brown over most of his body with a very dark brown head; the female is a gray-brown overall. Immature cowbirds look similar to the female. When the immature males molt, they can be blotched all over with black and darker brown on the body and head. The cowbird has a short bill and a short tail and measures from six to eight inches.

Cowbirds are primarily insect eaters and feed on our lawns. Occasionally they will come to bird feeders to eat the seeds and insects beneath them. Once in a great while they overwinter in the northern part of the United States eating birdseed.

The cowbird does not build a nest of its own; instead it lays its eggs in the nests of other birds. These eggs are white speckled with brown and hatch sooner than the eggs of the host birds. The young, which grow faster than the host young do, become very aggressive and will often crowd the host young out by demanding all the food from the foster parents. This behavior means that the nests of some of the birds we prefer to have in our neighborhoods are not successful.

It is believed that the cowbird learned this behavior of placing its eggs in other birds' nests because of its habit of following the buffalo to catch the insects the animal scared up. (Cowbirds feed the same way today, following cows and tractors.) Since buffaloes did not stay in one place very long, the cowbirds had to either travel back and forth to feed their young or learn to place their eggs in other birds' nests, letting them take care of the parental duties.

Purple Finch and House Finch, Female
page 105

Purple finches and house finches are both covered in the red bird section because the males are red. The females, which are both brown, are difficult to distinguish from each other. The female purple finch is a shorter, squatter bird than the female house finch. It has a definite cheek patch of gray or light brown with a white area above and beneath the eye. The female house finch has no facial pattern and is a basic gray. Both the females have light gray streaking on the breast. The house finch has a squared-off tail that is longer than the notched tail of the purple finch. So there are differences, but the best clue is to see the male with the female.

Purple finches are normally found in the eastern United States during the winter and during spring and fall migration. The house finch can be found in the entire eastern United States year round. It has become quite a common nesting bird and sometimes a serious pest at bird feeders because it drives away other small birds such as chickadees and goldfinches.

Indigo Bunting, Female and Immature Male
page 105

The male indigo bunting is discussed in the blue section. The female indigo bunting, a plain buffy brown, is a difficult bird to identify because it has no readily recognizable field markings. It is the same shape as the male indigo bunting and has the same conical, light gray-blue bill. Some of the feathers around the neck, on the wings, and under the tail may have a bluish tinge to them, but this is difficult to see unless you are close to the bird. The immature males have a similar appearance. When they begin to molt, they have a blotchy look as they change to their dark blue color. Habitat and association with the male is probably the best way to identify this female.

Red-winged Blackbird, Female

The female red-winged blackbird (see black birds) is a predominantly brown bird with light tan streakings throughout much of its body. It has a black eye stripe, a tan stripe above the eye, and a black head. The lower body is lighter in color than the upper body. Occasionally during breeding season the female will have a buff to pinkish buff throat. The easiest way to identify the female red-winged blackbird is by its size ($7^{1}/_{2}$ to $9^{1}/_{2}$ inches) and its sharp, pointed bill.

Mourning Dove
page 105

The mourning dove is the most common dove in the eastern United States. It is a brownish tan bird with a long pointed tail that exhibits white wing spots on the outer parts when it flies. Although not striking in color, the mourning dove is quite a pretty bird; at eleven to thirteen inches it is also a large one.

It is also a welcome addition to our backyard feeding station. In the summertime the mourning dove can be found there eating millet, sunflower, cracked corn, and thistle. Its mournful coo during the morning and evening hours is a familiar sound.

The mourning dove nests early in the spring, usually in a pine tree. The nest is made of sticks loosely placed on a platform or a horizontal branch. Two white eggs are laid that hatch in about two weeks. The young are fed regurgitated "mother's milk" by both the male and female and leave the nest in about two weeks. Two to five broods can occur during the summer.

• • • • • • • SPARROWS • • • • • • • •

Sparrows are considered little brown birds by most people, but they are actually easy to identify if you at least recognize that they belong in the sparrow family. They all have conical bills that are very strong; the sparrows use them to crack open seeds, although they also eat insects and berries.

Chipping Sparrow
page 106

The chipping sparrow is a common bird of our backyards, frequently nesting in small pine trees or shrubs. The easiest identifier is the way it sits on top of small trees or shrubs and gives a long trill or a series of "chips." It has a bright rusty cap, a black line through its eye, and a white stripe above the eye. It has a gray breast and a typical sparrow back of brown and black with little white wing bars. It is one of the smaller sparrows, only 5 to 5 1/2 inches.

The nest is placed in a pine tree, spruce, or arborvitae not far off the ground, perhaps three to six feet. The outer part of the nest is built of dead grasses and weeds and the inner cup is lined with hair and fine grasses. The chipping sparrow is especially fond of hair. The hair is so tightly woven that the nest can last for several seasons, even though it is only used by the bird for one. The eggs are a pale greenish blue and have various black and brown markings on them. The eggs are incubated by the female for about two weeks. The young leave the nest quickly, sometimes as early as eight days, but generally about ten. In a large portion of its territory the chipping sparrow will have more than one brood.

The chipping sparrow, or "chippy" as many people call it, is an enjoyable bird to have in your yard. It eats large amounts of insects as well as many weed seeds. Occasionally it will stay through part of the winter, and sometimes one will stay at a bird feeder throughout the season, although this is not common.

Song Sparrow
page 106

The song sparrow is a bit larger than the chipping sparrow, measuring between five and seven inches. It is characterized by the many streaks on its breast, often with a central black spot. The song sparrow has a light buff stripe above the eye, a dark line through the eye, and a very pronounced mustache or sideburn coming down from the bill. It is quite a tame bird and moves among people with little fear. It eats insects, seeds, and berries and is easily attracted to feeders.

The nest is built on the ground in thick tufts of grass, weeds, or shrubs. Usually five greenish white eggs are laid that are heavily marked with brown. The female sits on the nest about two weeks. As with the chipping sparrow, the nestlings leave in eight to ten days. Usually more than one brood is raised per year. Occasionally in the southern part of the territory there will be three broods. The song sparrow is welcome in our yards especially in early spring when it starts to sing.

Fox Sparrow
page 106

The fox sparrow is our largest sparrow at $6^1/2$ to $7^1/2$ inches. Its color patterns are similar to the song sparrow's except it is a rusty red all over with rusty red streakings on the breast and a central dark spot. It also has the same facial markings as the song sparrow. Its characteristic habit of scratching on the ground with its feet for food is a good way to identify it.

The fox sparrow nests in northern Canada but is a frequent visitor to the eastern United States during migration and to the southeast during winter. It will eat millet and other seeds beneath a feeder, rarely perching on the feeder unless it is a platform.

White-crowned Sparrow
page 106

The white-crowned sparrow is recognized by its black and white striped head and pinkish bill. It is about the same size as the fox sparrow, $6^1/2$ to $7^1/2$ inches.

The white-crowned sparrow nests in Canada. During migration it is a welcome addition at our bird feeding areas, eating sunflower and millet. They are found in the southern United States during winter; an occasional bird will stay in the northern states throughout the season.

House Sparrow
page 106

The house sparrow or English sparrow is actually not a sparrow. It is a weaver finch introduced into the United States from Europe in the early 1900s. It quickly became a very widespread bird. Although they are both brownish birds, the male and female look quite different. The male has a gray cap, a black

**House Sparrow,
continued**

bib, and a brownish swath through his eye; the side of his face is gray and white. The female is a duller brown and has no facial markings except for a buff-colored stripe above the eye and a light tan stripe through it. Both male and female measure six inches.

The house sparrow, a cavity nester, causes problems for other cavity-nesting birds such as the bluebirds and the purple martins because it occupies their preferred habitat. If bird houses are not readily available, it will use any openings such as those found in the eaves of buildings. Occasionally house sparrows build in open trees, especially evergreens like spruce and arborvitae. In places where buildings are heavily covered with vines, they will make a weaver nest in the shape of a large oval or ball with a small opening in the side of the nest cavity. Usually five eggs are laid. These are light in color, white or sometimes pale blue, with a few brown or gray markings on them. The eggs hatch in about fourteen days and the young birds leave in another two weeks.

The house sparrow is probably one of the most common birds we see at our feeders, especially in and around cities. It is a skittish bird, perhaps because it has been persecuted for many centuries. Even in the early 1900s the house sparrow had a two-cent bounty placed on it because it was so numerous and interfered with other cavity nesters. It does eat many insects and weed seeds and is therefore somewhat beneficial. Nevertheless, it is one of the few birds not protected by federal law at this time.

**American Tree
Sparrow**
page 106

The American tree sparrow can be found during the winter in the northern half of eastern North America. It nests in the upper tier of states and migrates down for the wintertime. The American tree sparrow is easily identified. It has a plain white breast with one central black spot. The mandibles on the bill are different colors: the lower mandible is yellow and the upper one is black.

American Tree Sparrow, continued

The American tree sparrow lives in coniferous forests in northern North America. It builds its nest out of grasses and small plant fibers. It lays four to five eggs that take about eleven days to hatch and another two weeks for the young to leave the nest. The American tree sparrow, like the junco, is a good addition to our bird feeding stations during the wintertime. It is quite a perky little bird. If you find tree sparrows in a field, they are quite noisy, and their calls back and forth to each other sound like so many fairy bells.

• • • • • • • **BLACK BIRDS** • • • • • • • •

Many birds have the color black included in their markings. Nevertheless, there are very few entirely black birds. That makes these few easily recognizable.

European Starling
page 107

The European starling is a short bird (7^1/2 to 8 inches) with a very long bill. The bill is bright yellow during the summertime and black during the winter. From a distance, the starling looks black, but on close inspection it has a purple or greenish iridescence to its feathers. It also has white spots that are very pronounced during the winter. The tail is short with a squared-off end. In flight the stocky starling is triangular in shape and flies in a straight, direct line unlike other blackbirds which fly with an undulating flight.

The starling, like the house sparrow, was introduced into the United States from Europe. It is a cavity nester, often getting into holes in the sides of buildings and thereby causing problems with louse infestations. It also has become a serious pest to other nesting birds because it takes away their nest cavities. The starling builds its nest of dead grasses, straw, twigs, and weeds. It lays four or five greenish blue to white eggs. The eggs hatch in about two weeks and the young fledge in about three weeks. The starling is found all over the United States, especially in cities where it can find many available nesting cavities.

**European Starling,
continued**

After the summer breeding season, starlings may congregate in flocks numbering from a few hundred birds to a few thousand. The starling can be found year round in most areas, though some individuals will migrate to different locations. Although it is not one of the mimic thrushes, the starling is adept at imitating a variety of other bird calls.

The starling is a beneficial bird as it eats lots of insects. Huge flocks of starlings may land on your lawn, nearly eating it devoid of insects in a short time. Even though it is beneficial, it is not a bird protected by federal law.

Common Crow or American Crow
page 107

The common or American crow is the largest of our black birds. It is easily recognized because it is entirely black with a black bill. It is also distinguished by its size: seventeen to twenty-one inches. It can be found in most areas where there are people, especially if there is food available. Crows have readily adapted to using man as a food source, feeding in suburbs and also in dumps. They will come to feeders if you have a good supply of suet, and even white bread will attract them. A good way to recognize the common crow of course is by its loud raucous call.

The crow is migratory but can be found in most parts of eastern North America during the entire year. The crow can be considered a beneficial bird because it does eat many insects. Occasionally it will cause problems to crops, especially corn.

The crow builds its nest high in a tree. It is made of sticks and twigs and lined with leaves, grasses, bits of plant material, and perhaps some string, yarn, and wool. Five to seven light green spotted eggs are laid and hatch in about two weeks. The young leave the nest somewhere between three and five weeks depending on the food availability and how many young need to be fed.

Common Grackle
page 107

The common grackle is a dark bird that appears black from a distance. If seen up close, however, it exhibits a purple iridescent sheen. It has a black bill and black legs similar to those of the crow, but it is a much smaller bird (eleven to fourteen inches) and has a yellow eye in contrast to the black eye of the crow. The tail is relatively long and in flight it looks like a V-shaped trough, as if it had a keel like a boat. The common grackle, or purple grackle as it is sometimes called, is an easy bird to spot walking across our lawns. It seems to move majestically with its long keeled tail dragging behind it.

Grackles sometimes nest by themselves but more often nest together in trees. A popular spot is in a group of trees such as evergreens and shrubs in city parks. The nests are bulky, made of twigs, leaves, and stalks of plants and lined with grass and finer plant material. Four to six eggs are laid that are a light green with brown markings. The eggs hatch in about fourteen days and the young are ready to leave the nest in an additional fourteen. Two broods are sometimes raised per year.

The common grackle is a good bird to have around because it eats lots of insects, especially in our lawns and gardens. It will also come readily to feeders, eating sunflower and millet. Those who don't want to feed grackles can use safflower in their bird feeders during the summer.

Grackles are very early migrators, congregating and moving about during the summer in huge flocks, beginning as early as late July. These flocks, numbering in the thousands, are made up of different blackbirds such as starlings, red-winged blackbirds, and cowbirds as well as grackles. They can be unnerving in the suburbs when they congregate in trees. Occasionally diseases are linked to these giant flocks because they roost in the same areas night after night, their droppings accumulating and covering the ground.

Cowbird
page 107

The male cowbird has a glossy brown-black body that can look either brown or black. It is described in detail in the brown bird section.

Red-winged Blackbird
page 107

The red-winged blackbird is an easily recognized bird in the eastern United States. It is all black with a red shoulder patch bordered with yellow. Sometimes this shoulder patch can be covered and only the small bit of yellow is visible. When the male displays during breeding season the red patch is very prominent. The female is a brown speckled bird with a buff stripe above the eye, a brown stripe through the eye, and a buff-colored throat. Immature males look similar to the females except they do show a slight red patch on the wings before molting later in the year. Red-wings measure between $7 \frac{1}{2}$ and $9 \frac{1}{2}$ inches.

The red-winged blackbird is one of the most numerous birds in the United States. Normally a nester in cattail marshes, the red-wing has adapted to suburban brush and fields. It has also taken over the millions of miles of cattail marshes in the ditches along super highways. An average of five to seven pairs of birds per mile can be found in these man-made habitats. In its normal habitat of the cattail marsh there may be three to five females nesting, but in the habitat of the suburban fields and shrubs, usually only one male and female nest.

In the spring breeding season the male tries to attract a female by sitting on top of a branch and puffing up his epaulets (the patches of red on his wings). He moves progressively higher and higher on the branch, calling repeatedly to challenge any other red-wing that might come into his territory.

A migratory bird in most of its range, the red-winged blackbird is one of the first to return in the springtime. The males begin arriving in February in many areas and the females follow a few weeks later. They will eat at your bird feeder during the springtime but not as often in the summer.

**Red-winged
Blackbird,
continued**

The nest is usually made of plant materials found nearby such as grasses, cattails, and weeds. The red-wing makes a cup woven between two stalks in the shrubs or cattails. The inside of the cup is lined with the finer parts of the cattail heads or grasses. Four or five pale blue eggs with squiggly lines on them are laid; they hatch in ten to twelve days and leave the nest in another ten to twelve. Two nestings can occur during one season.

CHAPTER · THREE

REPTILES AND AMPHIBIANS

Some representative of the reptile and amphibian groups can usually be found in our yards. Amphibians, such as frogs, toads, and salamanders, have a few characteristics that make them easy to distinguish from reptiles. They normally have smooth skin and go through a tadpole or nymph stage of development in water. Reptiles, on the other hand, have scaly dry skin and do not require water in a stage of their life cycle. Some examples are snakes, turtles, and lizards.

Amphibians are harmless to humans, although if certain kinds are eaten by a dog or a cat, they can cause gastric problems and sometimes death. Some snakes, however, are poisonous; fortunately, these species are not commonly found in our yards. All snakes, turtles, and lizards can bite and possibly cause infection. It is therefore wise to seek medical attention if any unusual circumstances concerning a bite arise. Normally these creatures are not aggressive and prefer to leave you alone. They bite in defense when they are startled or feel threatened.

Amphibians like moist habitats. This is one of the reasons they come out mostly in the evening and nighttime. Reptiles can readily be found during the day because they like to sun themselves. The scales of a reptile protect them from drying out, whereas the skin of the amphibian does not. Reptiles and amphibians are cold-blooded: their body temperatures fluctuate with their surroundings (as opposed to warm-blooded animals that maintain a constant temperature).

Reptile young may be born alive or they may be hatched from eggs that are placed in the ground. Amphibians must have water in which to lay their eggs; the eggs hatch into tadpoles and then develop into adults.

Reptiles and amphibians are usually an asset to our yard, rarely causing any damage. Most of them eat other living things such as insects, though the box turtle will eat some reachable berries.

Box Turtle
page 108

The land turtle that we most often encounter is the easily identified box turtle. It is between five and ten inches long. Both the shell and the body are bright

Box Turtle, continued

yellow with brown or black markings. The head and the legs are black all over with yellow markings. The box turtle's shell can be closed completely in both front and back because it is hinged at the bottom. The male has red eyes whereas the female's are brown. The box turtle does not have a very large range: there is usually no more than several hundred yards in a territory. It travels through this territory eating insects, berries, and plants. You can sometimes tell what the box turtle has been eating by the color of its face. When it eats strawberries or dewberries, for instance, the face will turn the color of the berries.

Box turtles live an extremely long time. Some people have recorded ages of fifteen to thirty years. But in some areas they are becoming endangered because people take them from the wild and keep them as pets.

• • • • • • • • • **TOADS** • • • • • • • • • •

Toads are amphibians that can stay out of water for long periods of time. During the hot part of the day they usually burrow into the ground or under a board or rock to keep out of the direct sun. The only time a toad normally goes near water is to lay eggs and occasionally, in a particularly dry summer, to soak up water in its skin.

A toad's skin, which is drier than that of frogs, is usually covered with warts. Toads have a parotoid or wart gland located behind the eye that exudes a bad-tasting liquid. This helps protect them from being eaten. A toad also has a number of spots on its skin and ridges on the head between the eyes. These spots and ridges help distinguish the different types of toads since their coloration can vary dramatically from brown and gray to orange and green and even yellow. Behind the eye there is usually a large ear called a tympanum. This ear is circular and likened to a drum head. Its shape, size, and location help identify the toad species.

The tadpole stages of toads and frogs will not be discussed here, because these are not normally found in yards but in ponds, lakes, and streams. The tadpoles can vary dramatically in size and color, ranging from one-quarter inch to over three inches long in the larger frogs. Tadpoles eat dead plants or plant material but adult frogs and toads eat insects and other small living animals.

American Toad

The American toad is normally two to four inches long. It is the most common toad in the northeastern United States. It has only one or two warts in each large brown or black spot on its back and sides. The parotoid gland or wart gland behind the eye is usually separated from the cranial crest. The cranial crest is L-shaped with one ridge very close to the eye on each side. Occasionally the L-shaped crest will have a small spur pointing toward the parotoid gland. The underside of the toad usually has numerous spots. The call of the American toad during mating season is a long varied trill lasting anywhere from a few seconds to almost a half minute.

Common Toad
page 108

The common toad, sometimes called the Woodhouse's toad or Fowler's toad, has more than two warts per large black spot on the back. The underside of the belly is usually devoid of spots or has one central black spot. There is a faint line running from head to tail on each side. The cranial crest on the common toad normally touches the wart glands behind the eye. Its call sounds like the bleat of a sheep. The common toad can be found over the entire eastern United States. It prefers a sandy habitat and can reach up to five inches in length.

Southern Toad
page 108

The southern toad is 1$1/2$ to 4 inches in length and is normally found in the southeastern United States. It is easily recognized because of the L-shaped cranial crests, which are very large and pronounced. These ridges also sport a spur and pronounced knobs, giving the effect of horns much like a horned toad. The male may have a dark throat. The southern toad usually has three or more warts per spot and the belly is less speckled than that of the American toad. The ear is somewhat elongated or oval. Occasionally the warts on the southern toad possess little spinelike points.

Tree frogs are relatively small frogs with moist, very thin skin. They are normally found in trees and shrubs around our yard. In the springtime, they have a loud, clear, melodious call.

Other common types of frogs are not mentioned here because they are not normally found in our yards. Their habitat is the edges of lakes and streams.

Squirrel Tree Frog
page 108

The squirrel tree frog is from 1 to 1 1/2 inches long. It commonly is green in color, but like most of the tree frogs it can change from green to gray to brown to match whatever it is sitting on. Normally there is a dark spot between the eyes no matter which color variation is present. Like the other tree frogs, it has suction cups on its feet that allow it to climb trees and hang onto branches and leaves. Its snout is short and somewhat pointed. The call is a short bark or quack that the frog repeats quite rapidly during breeding season. The noise resembles the scolding call of a squirrel.

The squirrel tree frog is found in the very southern part of the eastern United States. Whenever it rains or the air is very moist, squirrel tree frogs become more visibly abundant.

Green Tree Frog
page 108

The green tree frog is usually green or yellowish green and does not change as often to a brown or a gray color as do other tree frogs. It normally has a pronounced light-colored stripe along its side. The green tree frog resides in the southern United States and ranges from 1 1/4 to 2 1/2 inches long. The voice of the green tree frog is somewhat reminiscent of a bell. Some call it the bell frog or even the cowbell frog.

Gray Tree Frog
page 108

The gray tree frog, 1 1/2 to 2 1/2 inches, is probably the easiest tree frog to see in the northeastern United States. As its name indicates, this frog is usually gray, but it can also be a blotched green or brown

Gray Tree Frog, continued

depending on the surrounding habitat. The gray tree frog has highly variable markings on the back, unlike the squirrel and green tree frogs which are a solid color. Another identifying characteristic of the gray tree frog is a light spot, usually bordered with some type of dark color, beneath the eye. The inside surface of the hind legs is bright yellow. Although this frog is smooth skinned, the back often has a quantity of small warts.

The voice of the gray tree frog is similar to a very shortened version of the American toad: a loud trill done very quickly. Like the other tree frogs, this frog is rarely seen except in times of rain or heavy dew or at night.

• • • • • • • **LIZARDS** • • • • • • • •

Lizards are reptiles that have scaled skin, long tails, and four feet that have toes with toenails. They are generally very quick and lie in hiding to capture insects and other small animals. The two lizards that reside in the eastern United States are the anole and the skink.

Green Anole
page 108

The green anole is probably the most common lizard around our yards in the southern states. It can change color dramatically from brown to blotched greens and grays. Many people call the anoles the chameleons of North America. The most prominent feature of the green anole is the male's throat fan, a flap of skin that opens up from the throat and extends forward in a fan shape. This flap can be brightly colored from pink to brown to purple and fuchsia. The males display the fan during mating and also when they defend their territory. Anoles, which range from five to eight inches, can be found on many trees and shrubs in a yard.

Five-lined Skink
page 108

The five-lined skink is another lizard we may find in our yards. Skinks have long tails in comparison to the rest of their body. When the five-lined skink is young, its tail will be bluish in color. A breeding

Five-lined Skink,
continued

male exhibits a bright orange or reddish orange under the jaw. The five-lined skink is found through most of North America except in the far south and the extreme north. They are more commonly found in suburban areas that were at one time forested or sandy. Unlike typical lizards, which enjoy naps in the sun, they are very secretive and prefer shaded areas. Five-lined skinks measure from about five to eight inches long.

• • • • • • • • • **SNAKES** • • • • • • • •

Snakes are reptiles with scaled skin, long tails, and of course no legs. Snakes can often be found in yards, especially those with natural habitat such as shrubs, trees, or nearby fields. They like to sun themselves on fences, stones, and tree branches. Most snakes are not easily seen because they normally avoid humans if at all possible.

Snakes are quick but usually harmless. Most of the poisonous snakes are not found in a normal suburban situation. But all snakes you encounter should be handled with care or not at all, because they can bite. They all have sharp teeth that usually point backyard and tear the skin as you try to pull the snake off. Because they are animal eaters and their teeth are not clean, a bite can cause an infection.

Ring-necked Snake
page 109

Ring-necked snakes are easily identified. The underside is usually a bright yellow to orange; the upper body is generally a darker color: brown, gray, or black. If picked up, the ring-necked snake will secrete a few drops of musk, usually from its mouth. It is a very slender snake and is usually fifteen to twenty inches long. The ring-necked snake can be found through most parts of eastern North America. Very secretive, they are most often found by overturning rocks, logs, and similar objects. Ring-necked snakes like to feed on small salamanders, small frogs, and insects.

Corn Snake
page 109

Corn snakes are fairly long, ranging from two to four feet with records exceeding five feet. They are normally found only in the southern part of eastern North America. The corn snake belongs to the rat

**Corn Snake,
continued**

snake group and is sometimes called the red rat snake or the orange rat snake. The basic coloration is a yellowish orange all over with blotches of orangish brown outlined in black. Like the ring-necked snake it is relatively secretive and stays away from people. Corn snakes like rocky hillsides or stone walls where they hunt for rodents in their burrows. Although like the other rat snakes they can climb very well, they prefer not to do so. They can, however, climb trees and bushes very quickly if necessary. Like many of the rat snakes and blue racers, when they feel threatened they wiggle their tails in dry leaves to give the impression of a rattlesnake.

Milk Snake
page 109

Milk snakes range in length from one to four feet. They have somewhat the same coloration as the corn snakes, although a greater portion of their bodies is covered with the orange or brown-orange blotches outlined in black. The blotch on the head is generally triangular in shape.

Milk snakes are often found around old buildings, especially barns and corncribs. Long ago people used to think they milked the cows, but of course this isn't true. The grain in barns brings mice and rats, which the snakes eat. Because we have greatly eliminated most of the milking barns, cribs, and granaries, the milk snake is now seen more frequently around yards, particularly if attracted by mice and rats found around spilled birdseed or dog food. They will also eat other types of snakes as well as other reptiles, small birds, and amphibians. Milk snakes are not especially secretive and are often visible along the edges of buildings, rock piles, and wherever rodents might be. They are skittish but can become accustomed to people.

Garter Snake
page 109

Garter snakes, which measure from one to four feet, have black and yellow stripes running from head to tail making them easily identifiable. Occasionally

Garter Snake, continued

there are other colors mixed with the yellow stripes such as orange and red.

Garter snakes like a habitat of tall grasses and shrubs. They often hibernate in huge colonies numbering from about fifteen to over a hundred. In the spring one can sometimes spot twenty or thirty garter snakes sunning themselves along a grassy bank near the opening of their den. They eat lots of insects, amphibians, and small reptiles. Garter snakes bear their young alive and quite often stay together as a family for a few months. They frequently live near water even though they are not true water snakes. They even have been known to eat fish.

Hog-nosed Snake
page 109

The hog-nosed snake can be found throughout the entire eastern part of North America except for the northernmost parts of Maine. It rarely grows more than two feet long, although some records go up to three feet. The somewhat fat hog-nosed snake gets its name from its upturned nose. It has an overall tan or orangish hue that can be very light in sandy habitats. Blotches of black or brown are scattered across the body. It prefers to eat toads, though it also feeds on other small animals and insects.

The hog-nosed snake is sometimes called the blow-nosed snake or the bluff snake because it tries to intimidate people. It does this by opening its mouth and hissing or blowing. If this doesn't work it will rattle its tail in dry leaves, pretending it is a rattlesnake. When this has no result it will try a false strike, though it usually does not open its mouth. If you are still around and obviously not scared, it will turn belly side up, indicating that it is dead and should be left alone. If you pick it up it will secrete a musky odor on your hands.

Smooth Earth Snake
page 109

Earth snakes are usually less than one foot long. They are usually devoid of any special markings and are uniform dark brown to gray-brown or black,

Smooth Earth Snake, continued

except the underside which may be white or have some color. Neither the nose nor the tail is very pointed. Earth snakes are very secretive and spend most of their lives in an acre or two underground. They rarely come out unless their burrow floods or becomes too moist. They feed mostly underground on earthworms and insect grubs. Most often we encounter the earth snakes when digging our gardens, especially in a new subdivision where previously there was forest.

Black Snake

The black snake, also called the rat snake or black rat snake, can generally be found from the Great Lakes south. The rat snake can reach lengths exceeding eight feet but is more commonly around six feet long. It is predominately black with a white underchin or throat. The young hatchlings are strikingly patterned with grays and blacks. Some of this pattern may be faintly evident in the adult black rat snakes.

The female black snake lays its eggs during mid-summer and in about two months the eggs hatch. The young snakes are able to feed for a short time before they go into hibernation during the fall.

Though they generally feed on rodents, black rat snakes are quite adept at climbing trees and shrubs and can go quite high in a tree to captrue small birds and raid bird nests.

King Snake

The king snake can also be found south of the Great Lakes throughout the eastern part of the United States. This snake has a striking pattern of light gray stripes over a black body. It grows to about six or seven feet. King snakes are quite beneficial because they eat many insects and small rodents. The female lays its eggs during the early part of the summer and they hatch in roughly six to eight weeks.

CHAPTER FOUR

CREATURES IN MOIST PLACES

Many creatures are very dependent upon moisture. During the hot part of the day these creatures will hide under leaves, rocks, logs, or anywhere they can keep themselves out of the hot sun. The animals discussed here fall into different categories: mollusks, crustaceans, millipedes, centipedes, and worms.

Striped Forest Snail
page 110

The shell of the striped forest snail is relatively flat with no dramatic peak in the front. It has alternate bands of brown and tan starting at the lip and going inward. The snails range in size from 3/4 to 1 1/4 inches. As the snail grows, the shell gets larger as well. The body of the striped forest snail is beige in color.

Snails have a long false foot that they glide upon. They have two antennae at the end of which their eyes are located. Forest snails and land snails are relatively fast and usually leave behind them a trail of slime exuded by the foot. The striped forest snail is easily recognized by its orange slime trail. It eats mostly plants and dead plant material, although once in a great while it feeds on dead animal material. The striped forest snail can be found in yards or wherever trees are fairly abundant. They cannot survive in a dry area or an area that is disturbed frequently such as a garden.

White-lipped Forest Snail
page 110

The white-lipped snail also can be found in our suburban neighborhoods wherever there are trees available. This snail's shell, from 1 to 1 3/4 inches long, is beiger than the striped forest snail's and is almost devoid of striping. It has a lip on the front that is flared and white in color. The body is a lighter tan than the striped snail's. Neither of the two forest snails do significant damage to our gardens. They provide a food source for birds and small mammals.

Common Slug
page 110

Slugs can range in color and size dramatically. The common slug we find in our garden is usually from one-quarter to three-quarters of an inch long and is black or dark gray in color. Slugs are very similar to snails. They have antennae or stalks and the same body shape as the snail, but with no visible shell. The large common slugs can be quite varied in size, ranging up to three or four inches long. They have dramatic color markings from gray and brown to almost orange. Like the snails, slugs usually leave behind a slime trail. During dry parts of the year, slugs go into summertime hibernation called *estivation* when they curl up in a cocoon underground. They are more prominent during the moist spring and fall months when heavy dew allows them to travel for longer periods of time.

During very wet, rainy summers, huge slugs can be found all around the yard. Slugs are predominately plant eaters and can cause dramatic injury to garden plants, especially vegetable crops. Occasionally they will damage shrubs and ornamental plant foliage also. To control slugs, provide a place for them to hide during the daytime such as a flat rock or board that is quite moist and placed in the perimeters of where the slug damage occurs. During the daytime pick up the rock or board and scrape the slugs off. Another way to dispose of them is to place a shallow dish of beer or some type of fermented liquid near where slug damage is occurring. The slugs will be attracted to it, crawl into it, and drown. If you prefer to use insecticide, it is most often effective to spray during the night or early morning when the slugs are moving about.

Earthworm
page 110

Earthworms are segmented worms from two to eight inches in length. There are a number of different kinds ranging from the common leaf worm to the earthworm to nightcrawlers. Earthworms lack eyes but are very sensitive to light, motion, and moisture. Most of them have a band across their back about thirty to forty segments from the front that is used in mating.

Earthworms are soft-bodied and long. Each segment has tiny hairs called *setae*. These allow it to brace itself in holes against a predator's tugs. It is very difficult to pull an earthworm out unless you can keep enough pressure on it to relax its muscles.

Probably no creature does as much for our soil, yards, and gardens as does the earthworm. It turns the soil over every couple of years. It also aerates it, allowing water and air to get to the roots of plants. Earthworms burrow back and forth in the ground eating dead and decaying plant material and providing the earth with nutrients. It is recommended that insecticides not be soaked into lawns because they will kill the earthworms.

Besides being good for the soil, earthworms provide an excellent food source for many other animals, especially birds. In the spring earthworms are more apt to come to the surface because of the spring rains. They also come to the surface to mate.

Earthworms lay several hundred tiny packets of eggs in the soil. The eggs hatch and the small worms begin their underground life. If you have few earthworms in your soil you can purchase some where worms are raised for bait.

The nightcrawler is our largest earthworm, sometimes growing past eight inches. It is a bit darker in color on the dorsal or upper surface. The nightcrawler is an easy worm to capture for fish bait in the early springtime when it comes out at night to feed and seek a mate.

Sow bug and Pill bug
page 110

The sow bug and the pill bug are crustaceans that live on land. They breathe through gills at the base of their legs and therefore need moisture to live. So you won't see them out during the middle of the day in the hot sun. During the last part of the summertime sow bugs and pill bugs can become quite abundant especially under pots, boards, and rocks where there is a great deal of moisture.

These crustaceans can grow up to one-half inch long, though the sow bug is shorter and squatter than the pill bug. Their gray or black bodies are segmented and they have many legs and short, backward-bent antennae. They have the characteristic habit of rolling up into a pill or ball when frightened. They primarily eat dead plant and animal material, so they are not damaging to anything we have in our yards.

Millipede
page 110

The sow bugs and pill bugs should not be confused with millipedes, though all three are segmented arthropods. Millipedes are long, roundish creatures with two pairs of legs per segment. Some of the millipedes can be quite colorful, ranging from dark brown to orange to maroon. They eat mostly plant material and can measure one-half to four inches in length; the longer millipedes are usually found in the south.

Dead and decaying plants predominate in the millipede's diet. When frightened, they roll up into a ball much like a coil or a snail shell. This is their best protection since they cannot run very quickly, in spite of all those legs. They can also give off a disagreeable odor and in some cases even spit up a lacquerlike substance.

Centipede
page 110

The centipede has one pair of legs per segment and is quite fast. In comparison to the house centipede discussed in chapter five, the centipedes we find in our backyards generally have shorter legs and flat-

**Centipede,
continued**

ter bodies because they live under rocks, leaves, logs, and any kind of lawn litter. Like their indoor cousins they are poisonous and capture other insects and living creatures by biting them. Centipedes can range from one-half to three inches in length. They generally feed at night so you will probably not see them moving about.

The centipede and millipede are easy to tell apart. Centipedes have flat bodies whereas millipedes have round bodies. Centipedes have two legs per segment and millipedes have four. Centipedes eat other living things such as insects, snails, and earthworms, sometimes even catching larger invertebrates. Millipedes eat only dead plants and therefore need neither a fast pace nor a poisonous bite. Both millipedes and centipedes can be found in our yards in most any moist area.

CHAPTER FIVE

INSECTS, SPIDERS, AND THEIR KIN

"Bugs" are what most people call anything that is small and creeps, crawls, or flies. This chapter deals with these so-called bugs and includes insects, spiders, and their relatives.

Insects, found worldwide, make up the largest number of creatures in the world with over a million different species. All insects have six legs, and winged insects usually have two pairs of wings. The young of many insects are called larvae, worms, or caterpillars; both at this stage and as adults they can cause major damage to plants and household items. Some insects also eat farm crops. But others are extremely beneficial as pollinators, such as bees and butterflies, and scavengers, such as maggots and dung beetles.

Some homeowners plant their gardens with insects in mind. Use of ladybird beetles and praying mantises as garden predators is becoming common, as is planting flowers for butterflies.

Insects usually have one of two life cycles. One life cycle includes four stages—the egg, the larva (caterpillar), the pupa (cocoon), and the adult. The other has only three stages—the egg, the immature, and the adult; the immature stages look just like small adults except that they generally have large heads and lack wings.

Insects in our backyard and home can come in many different colors, forms, and sizes. Most of them are not dangerous, but if you are bitten or stung, it is wise to seek professional medical attention. If you have numerous stinging insects where you live, it is wise to find out if you're allergic *before* you're stung.

Occasionally flies, ticks, and mosquitoes can cause or carry diseases. Again, be aware of what might be prevalent in your territory. For example, the deer tick ixodes, a small tick in the eastern United States and other parts of the country, can cause Lyme disease. This disease is easily controlled if caught early, but can cause some serious side effects if it is allowed to take its course.

Prevention is the best way to avoid problems with insects that bite or sting. Measures such as insect repellents and protective clothing work well. Many of these insects bite and sting only as a mechanism of defense. Therefore, while picking flowers and working in your yard, be careful where you place your hands. Make insects aware that you are nearby so they have a chance to escape before you put them into a position where they have to retaliate. The only insects that seek you out are mosquitoes, horse flies, ticks, and chiggers. Wasps normally like to leave you alone, as do the ants.

Insects come into our homes for one reason—food. If you eliminate the food source or block their access to it, the insects will in most cases cease to be a problem. If this does not work more drastic measures must be taken, which usually means killing them. This can be as simple as hitting them with a flyswatter or rolled-up newspaper, or you may have to resort to an insecticide for more persistent problems. In case of pesticides, try and identify the problem insect and seek the advice of a garden center or hardware store to provide you with the proper spray or powder. If you have infestations of termites, carpenter ants, or wood beetles, it is best to seek the services of a professional exterminator.

Although some insects are pests, learning about them and collecting them can be educational and enjoyable. Insects, spiders, and their kin are all around you. The following are some of the ones you are most likely to see.

BUGS

Grasshopper
page 115

Grasshoppers, sometimes called locusts, are green or brown in color. They generally have short antennae, large heads, and extremely large rear jumping legs. They are one to two inches in length. The front wings are leathery but the hind wings or underwings are filmy. Grasshoppers are basically leaf eaters, feeding on grasses, trees, and shrubs. They lay individual eggs that overwinter in the ground. The young look very similar to the adults when they hatch except for a very large head, pronounced hind jumping legs, and a small abdomen. The grasshoppers go through a gradual metamorphosis of five or six molts, growing wing pads and then wings. By midsummer, the adult grasshopper has acquired wings that allow it to fly.

Some grasshoppers have long antennae and are called long-horned grasshoppers. These are more common in trees and shrubs at the edge of your yard.

Grasshoppers can be a serious pest in a garden, especially in areas where grasses are not prolific.

They will feed on leafy plants such as spinach, chard, and other greens, seldom damaging plants like the tomato. A good way to control grasshoppers is to keep your lawn short, thereby eliminating their food supply and preventing a population buildup.

Cricket
page 111

Related to the grasshopper, crickets have large hind legs for jumping or hopping, long antennae, and four wings. The heads are large and flat-sided with big eyes. The front wings are leathery and the back or underwings are filmy and fanlike; only the back wings are used in flying. Crickets can be black or brown and eat food crumbs and scraps, preferring flour and cereal products. Young look like adults except they have no wings. Although not a serious household pest, the cricket's constant chirping, which it produces by rubbing its wings together, can be quite annoying. Control is similar to that for cockroaches.

Katydid
page 114

Katydids are grasshopperlike insects from $1/2$ to $1^1/2$ inches long. They are predominantly green, and their fore wings look like leaves. This is their protective coloration, since katydids are mostly found eating the leaves of trees and shrubs. Katydids have antennae that are nearly as long as their bodies. They sing during the late summer with their persistent "katy-did, katy-did, katy-did" call. If the temperature gets colder, they may just say "katy-did" once very slowly. Katydids make these sounds by rubbing their wings together.

As in most of the grasshopper species, katydids overwinter as eggs under the ground or on leaves and twigs that have fallen to the ground. Young katydids look similar to adults except they have no wings, are much smaller, and their large heads look like they need bodies to grow up behind them. As summer progresses they molt many times, first getting wing pads and eventually wings. Once mature, they can make the katy-did sound.

Not a serious pest of trees, katydids are a fun insect to have around. They sometimes appear suddenly at night on window screens. Katydids are easy to study because they do not jump or fly very readily; they probably think their protective green-leaf coloration will keep them from being seen.

Praying Mantis
page 114

Praying mantises are related to grasshoppers and crickets. They have huge forelegs that they fold in front of their bodies; these folded forelegs make them look as if they were praying. Actually they are waiting in ambush for other insects to come by. When one does go past, a mantis grasps its prey with its spiny front feet and eats it bite by bite. The praying mantis has a large head with two large eyes. The head can swivel back and forth enabling the mantis to look both behind it and from side to side (though the mantis stays practically motionless while waiting for insects to come). Praying mantises can be green or brown; they use these colors to hide themselves in grasses, trees, and shrubs. The North American mantis is native to the United States and is generally two to four inches long. Introduced species of praying mantis can reach lengths of six to seven inches.

The female lays an egg case on a stick, twig, or weed. The egg case looks like a patch of frothy plastic.

Praying mantises are good insects to have in your garden because they eat damaging insect pests. Many garden centers and garden catalogs sell praying mantis egg capsules to place around your garden. Do not overdo these egg capsules, however, for praying mantises are cannibalistic and very hungry when they hatch. They will eat each other. Once you have established a praying mantis population, don't mow or till your soil in the fall. This helps keep the population self-sustaining.

Cockroach
page 111

This relative of the cricket and grasshopper is the scourge of homeowners, contaminating food and producing nasty odors. Cockroaches may be reddish brown, brown, or black. They have flattened bodies from one-half to two inches long and long, thin antennae. Adults have four wings but prefer to run rather than fly, scurrying into any crack or crevice. Because they have gradual metamorphosis, the young look like miniature adults, and a variety of sizes are usually present. Other names for this insect are the water bug and Croton bug.

Eliminating food sources and hiding places will help rid the house of roaches, but they can live a long time without food. Ask your garden center or hardware store about a good program for removal. Be sure to apply the insecticides to all cracks and crevices the roaches frequent. Repeated treatment usually is needed because egg capsules, which take fourteen days to hatch, are not affected by sprays. Some roaches have become resistant to common pesticides so repeated fumigation by a professional may be necessary. Roaches are more common in warm climates, but man's artificial warm climates, our homes, have allowed them to be found anywhere humans can be found.

Stink Bug
page 113

Stink bugs are also called shield bugs, because their body shape resembles a shield that a gladiator might have used in Roman times. Although they can vary in color from brown, green, or black to the pretty harlequin bug that is orange, black, and tan, they all have the same distinctive shape. Normally the stink bug is colored somewhat similarly to the plant that it infests or uses as a host. Stink bugs usually average about one-half inch in length. Their antennae are not terribly long, usually about twice the length of the head. Stink bugs belong to the order Hemiptera, which means "half wings." When they fly you will notice that the front wing is partially leathery and partially filmy or semitransparent.

Young stink bugs look similar to the adults except they do not have as developed a wing and of course are smaller. They go through gradual metamorphosis, as do grasshoppers and praying mantises.

Stink bugs are true bugs: that is, they belong to the group of insects called bugs. This is a large group, many of which are plant pests. The true bugs, stink bugs included, are insects that suck plant juices with sucking mouth parts. This mouth or proboscis looks like a small straw or tube. Stink bugs and other true bugs can become serious garden pests, although not as serious as weevils.

The stink bug is, as its name indicates, a bug that emits an odor. While picking fruits such as raspberries, you may pop one into your mouth and experience a terrible taste—this is from the odor of the stink bug. Most predators such as birds and praying mantises do not seem to be bothered by the odor stink bugs emit when disturbed.

Box Elder Bug
page 112

The box elder bug is related to the stink bug or true bugs. It has the typical triangular shield behind the head that the true bugs have. Box elder bugs can be found anywhere in North America where box elder trees are grown, because the main staple of their diet is box elder leaves. This bug is just under one-half inch long. Its body is black with orange markings and its head is entirely black. The thorax has an orange stripe down the center on each side and orange patterns on the wing.

True bugs have gradual metamorphosis in which they go through stages when they look exactly like adults but without wings. Since they feed on box elder leaves, they are not a pest in our gardens. Unless found in great numbers they do not harm the trees either. They overwinter as adults, which does cause some problems. They often get into buildings during the fall and again in the spring when the weather starts to warm up.

Leafhopper

Leafhoppers, long, slender insects that hop from leaf to leaf, are related to the true bugs. Leafhoppers are quite pretty. Their fore wing is entirely leathery and very brightly colored, often with stripes of green, blue, orange, yellow and black. They are about one-quarter inch long. Leafhoppers have sucking mouth parts and, as their name indicates, they hop about sucking the sap from the leaves and plant stems. They can fly as well as hop. Leafhoppers can be a serious pest in trees, shrubs, and vegetables around our yard. They not only cause problems because they suck the sap out of the plants, but they also can carry diseases from one plant to another.

One particular leafhopper does not usually produce wings. It is called the spittle bug. The spittle bug lives in a mass of foam, which looks just like spit, at the base of a plant leaf or in a stem. Within this protective foam, which hides it from birds, the spittle bug sucks sap from the plant stem.

Aphid

Aphids are related to the leafhoppers. They are small insects usually less than one-quarter inch long. Aphids go through a number of different stages. The stage we are most familiar with is the nymph stage, in which they lack wings. Aphids are green most of the time, but can vary in color from orange to black to yellow.

Aphids are usually found at the very tip of the new growth on green plants. Because of their great numbers, they can cause serious damage to ornamental plants by sucking the juices from the new growth. They also transmit diseases. Fortunately, many insects feed upon aphids, such as the praying mantis and the ladybird beetle. Some ants tend aphids, treating them as we might treat cattle. They stroke the aphids to make them produce a type of juice that the ants eat. They also transport their "herd" underground during the winter to protect the aphids from the cold.

Aphid,
continued

Aphids normally overwinter as eggs. Only wingless females will hatch from the eggs that were laid the fall before; these in turn will produce tremendous numbers of offspring, often generating six to ten different broods during the summer. It is only during the fall that normal males and females develop. They mate, and their eggs produce the following spring's brood of female aphids. Many types of aphids are very specific to the plant host they infect, such as rose aphids, garden vegetable aphids, and aphids on different types of trees, such as apple and plum aphids.

Cicada
page 114

Cicadas are related to the leafhoppers and the aphids. The cicada is a fairly large insect ranging from $1^1/2$ to 2 inches long. The cicada produces what is probably the most common sound we hear in late summer: a loud buzz or hum coming from the treetops. They rub their wings together to make this buzzing noise. Cicadas are sometimes called locusts, although they are not at all related to them.

They spend most of their lives underground as nymphs, which look similar to the adult but with no wings. The nymph emerges from the ground, attaches itself to a tree, and breaks through its shell, emerging with a pair of wings that gradually unfurl. (The shell remains stuck to the tree until disturbed by rain or birds.) Often while the wings are unfurling and drying it will crawl further up the tree. In a very short time, fifteen to twenty minutes, it will be able to fly about. After the cicada emerges from its shell it is usually bright green, taking on black and other dark colors as it gets older. The wings are clear or semitransparent with borders of green in the veins.

Some cicadas are periodic, living underground as long as seventeen years in the nymph stage. The nymphs feed on the sap from the rootlets and roots that they find underground, but do little damage to trees and plants unless they are in great numbers. Once the adult emerges, it calls for a mate and then lays its eggs on a new or young twig of the host tree. This frequently kills or deforms the twig. As the eggs hatch, the young drop to the earth and start the life cycle over again by burrowing underground.

Adult cicadas do not live very long once they've emerged and have full flight—usually less than a month, sometimes only a few days. Since cicadas are loud, they are easily preyed upon by birds. A specialized wasp called the cicada killer also takes its toll. The cicada killer is a large black and yellow wasp, similar to the yellow jacket except five times as large. It will sting the cicada, bury it underground, and lay an egg with it. When the wasp larva hatches, it will have something to eat. Cicadas are not very damaging to trees and shrubs in our yard except for the occasional damage to the tips of branches where the eggs are laid.

Cicadas are sometimes called harvest flies. Since they are usually heard during the last part of summer on hot days—the dog days of summer— another name for them is the dog day harvest fly.

Mayfly
page 114

Mayflies are found only in areas where water is nearby. They spend most of their lives as nymphs in streams, lakes, and ponds. The larvae, which are shaped like the adult mayfly except they do not have wings, live in the water for up to three years. They have gills that look like tiny feathers on the abdomen and have three tails. As the larva matures, it crawls up on a stem or a piece of grass emerging from the water. It then breaks open its shell and the adult mayfly leaves the water. It takes only a short time for the wings to be pumped up and to dry out. The mayfly is a delicate insect with triangular wings, very filamentous and transparent, held above the body. It sits on four legs with its two front legs pointing forward as if it were praying. The abdomen has two long tails projecting from it. Colors can be anywhere from a smoky gray to black to a very light beige, and the size can be anywhere from under one-half inch to two inches long.

When the mayflies emerge, they do so in great numbers and can be found almost anyplace in our yard. They are sexually immature the first day they emerge and go through another molt. They then will mate, lay their eggs, and die. Fishermen are very attentive to the occurrence of the mayfly hatch because the fish feed voraciously on the larvae as they get close to the surface. Trout and other fish also feed on the adults when they come back to the pond to lay their eggs, dipping their ovipositors into the water. Many fishermen tie flies to imitate the mayfly. Mayfly adults do no harm to our gardens because they do not eat. On rare occasions, mayflies become numerous enough to cause loss of visibility by flying into your car windshield.

Dragonfly and Damselfly
page 114

Dragonflies and damselflies can be found in our yards if we are near some body of water such as a lake, stream, or river. The larvae of dragonflies and damselflies live in ponds or streams feeding on other invertebrates and insects. Sometimes dragonfly larvae even take small fish and tadpoles. The larvae are probably one of the most voracious larvae in the water, feeding upon anything that moves that they can capture. The adult dragonfly has somewhat the same eating habits, except that it must catch things that fly because it is too slow on foot. When it is time to emerge, the nymph crawls up on grass, sticks, or leaves that are above the water and breaks through its skin. It unfurls four wings that are clear or transparent containing many veins and sometimes spots. Dragonflies can be anywhere from $1^1/2$ to 3 inches long. They generally have large eyes and long narrow abdomens and their wings point straight out from the body.

One way to distinguish between dragonflies and damselflies is the position the wings are in when they are at rest. The dragonfly's wings are stretched

Dragonfly and Damselfly, continued

out flat, whereas a damselfly folds its wings up over its back. Generally, damselflies are smaller and more delicate looking. They also tend to have greater color variations in the wings, anywhere from black to spotted black, gray, and blue to green in color. Both give off metallic colors of greens and blues when seen close, especially around the head. The dragonflies and damselflies have very short antennae if noticeable at all. The eyes of both dragonflies and damselflies are quite large, producing a characteristic menacing look.

Adult dragonflies are sometimes called devil's darning needles or mosquito hawks, because they capture mosquitoes. Large adult dragonflies can give a bit of a bite if you handle them too carelessly. If you live near water or if you have a pond or watering station in your backyard, it's fun to watch the dragonflies and damselflies dip their abdomen and ovipositor into the water leaving behind one egg each time. Neither fly is at all harmful to any of the plants in our yards. In fact they are quite beneficial because they eat many insects, both in the water and in flight.

Mosquito
page 116

A mosquito is about one-quarter inch in size or a little longer. Mosquitoes, related to the fly, have only two wings. Where the second pair of wings should be, they have two tiny clubs. The antennae are usually plumy and the female has piercing or biting mouth parts with which to draw blood from its prey. Mosquitoes in certain parts of the world have had a dramatic influence on populations, carrying diseases like malaria and yellow fever. Fortunately, in North America and especially in the eastern United States, these diseases are uncommon or even nonexistent. Occasionally encephalitis, which is carried by mosquitoes, may be a problem in certain parts of the United States.

Only the female mosquito bites. The best way to protect yourself from mosquitoes is to apply an insect repellent that includes the insect-repelling chemical called DEET. There are a number of different brands on the market. Apply liberally over the clothing, avoiding skin if at all possible. The next best way to control mosquitoes is by eliminating their breeding habitat. Mosquito larvae are aquatic and the female lays its eggs on or in the water. The eggs hatch into larvae that feed in the pond and eventually turn into pupae, which are comma-shaped. They then hatch as adult mosquitoes. This life cycle takes a very short time, from a few days to only a week or so. By eliminating places for the mosquitoes to breed, you can decrease the number of mosquitoes in your backyard. This means making sure the eave troughs drain properly and no buckets of water are sitting around. Check your yards carefully, as even tire swings are potential places for mosquitoes to breed. The process of draining major swamps is no longer recommended because of the loss of habitat for other species. Normally the mosquitoes that are found in these swamps are not a serious pest to suburban neighborhoods.

Horse Fly
page 116

As with all flies, the horse fly has only two wings. These are clear, filmy wings with no spots on them. Where the back wings should be there are two stubs with clubs on the end. Horse flies are black to dark gray in color. They have the typical fly shape with a large head, small antennae, and a large black thorax and abdomen. They can measure up to one inch long.

Like mosquitoes, the females are the only ones that bite or suck blood. Instead of piercing mouth parts they have what are called rasping mouth parts. This means that the fly has to sit on its prey for some time before it can pierce the skin and draw blood. The prey usually feels the pain and chases the fly away before too much damage occurs.

The males of the horse fly feed on flowers. Like the mosquito, the larvae of the horse fly live in

Horse Fly,
continued

ponds and streams. The adults also are usually found near these swamps and ponds, although they can travel good distances. Horse flies aren't as common as they used to be when there were more cattle and horses, but they can at times be seen in our suburbs. Insect repellent will work with these flies, although long clothing would probably deter them just as well if not better. The horse fly does not usually put its eggs in small bodies or containers of water as does the mosquito; it needs ponds, marshes, lakes, or streams.

House Fly
page 111

The house fly has only two clear membranous wings with two club-like appendages where the back two wings should be. It has a large head with huge, reddish, compound eyes. It measures between one-eighth and one-quarter inch long. House flies are the most common flying insect in our homes. They eat any foodstuff open to the air. They are especially fond of sweet and decaying things. They lay their eggs on any food, including dead animals, on which they can land. The eggs hatch into larvae called maggots and feed on this food for two to ten days. They then pupate and a few days later emerge as adult flies.

One of the prime carriers of disease, house flies should be rigidly controlled. The best and easiest way is by using door and window screens. Pyrethrum sprays also work well if food and utensils can be covered to prevent contamination.

Earwig
page 111

A lot of myths have surrounded this little insect. The earwig does *not* crawl into the ears of sleeping people as one myth states. (This myth is the source of its name.) Actually it doesn't even like people, though the formidable-looking pincers on the abdomen as well as its aggressive attitude scare away many an intruder.

Earwigs are $1/4$ to $1^1/4$ inches long and a shiny reddish brown to dark brown in color. Their shiny bodies may cause us to liken them to beetles, but actually they are quite soft-bodied and are not related to beetles at all. Adult earwigs have long knobby antennae and leathery wings, but they do not often fly. The pincers of the male are curved, but the female's are relatively straight. Some scientists believe the pincers might aid in mating, but this has not been substantiated. Although they can give you a pinch if handled, they are not dangerous. Besides using their pincers to defend themselves, earwigs can emit a foul-smelling tarlike liquid when irritated.

Earwigs are common in dark, damp places. Usually they are found under litter, stones, grasses, boards, flower pots, bark, or any place that keeps them protected and moist. They feed at night on plants, food waste, and small insects.

Earwigs have a simple metamorphosis or life cycle, which means the young resemble the adults when hatched (except that they lack wings). They then go through a series of molts, increasing the length of their antennae and wings until they reach maturity. Females are very protective of their eggs and young, taking care of them until the young are able to fend for themselves.

Why do we have so many earwigs around during certain years? Because both adults and eggs overwinter in the ground or in some other protected space. When we have relatively mild winters, the amount of earwigs lost to winter kill is lessened. This allows for a greater "start up" population in the spring. Two generations are normal each summer. Although they are unnerving, earwigs can be quite beneficial. They eat many smaller insects, especially aphids, from plants, thereby reducing plant damage. Their main diet, however, is vegetation, so they can cause some minor damage to crops and gardens.

Centipede and Millipede
page 110

Centipedes are long, flat creatures with numerous legs. (Their name means "one hundred feet.") They have one pair of legs per segment and are very fast runners. The centipedes we find in our homes have legs that are long and fine, resembling those of daddy longlegs. Centipedes have antennae and they also have poison glands, which they use to poison prey they have captured. The centipedes we find outside usually have shorter legs and flatter bodies and are not as quick. Centipedes' poisonous bites can be painful but are not very dangerous to humans.

Although unnerving, centipedes are good creatures to have around in our homes because they eat other pests including baby cockroaches and silverfish. They should not be confused with millipedes ("a thousand feet"), which have rounder bodies and two pair of legs per segment, move very slowly, and curl up in a ball when disturbed. Millipedes eat only plant material and are usually found outside the home, unless a house is moist and contains mold, fungus, or plant material they can eat.

Centipedes are called thousand-leggers whereas millipedes are called hundred-leggers, probably because the centipede is much quicker than the millipede even though it has fewer legs per segment. Males of both species will sometimes build a small web of silk exuded from special glands for the purpose of attracting a female or holding eggs or sperm. They normally range in size from one-quarter inch to three inches, though in the tropical parts of the United States, some centipedes and millipedes can reach up to five- and six-inch lengths.

Silverfish and Firebrat
page 111

Silverfish and firebrats are fast-running, soft-bodied, flat insects found around dark, warm, moist places. They can become household pests. They measure between one-quarter and one-half inch long and are tapered from head to tail with long, threadlike antennae and three bristles for tails; for this reason they are sometimes called bristletails. Silverfish have a silver glint to their body scales, whereas the firebrat is brown. Other than color they are the same.

Both eat starch, glue, cereals, and scraps of food. Limiting their food sources, including damp, moldy places, will help control them, but they can remain alive for months without food. Neither of these insects will remain long in a completely dry environment. Your garden center or hardware store can recommend an insecticide for use around foodstuffs.

Flea
page 111

These small, brown, wingless insects are found as parasites on mammals and birds. Their flat bodies allow them to weave through hair or feathers with ease. Fleas also can jump great distances. Because of their hard bodies, fleas are difficult to squash or kill. They are also so small, only one-quarter inch at the largest, that they are often not detected. Watch for excessive scratching by pets and small itchy bumps on your skin.

The adult lays its eggs in the lint or dust particles found where animals sleep. The larvae feed on organic matter such as animal hair and dead skin. The adult feeds on the blood of the animal. A prime carrier of disease, fleas must be controlled. Flea collars, shampoos, and sprays are necessary for pets in addition to well cleaned bedding areas.

Black Carpenter Ant
page 111

Like all ants, the black carpenter ant has a slender or constricted waist between its front and rear body and an antenna that is bent like an elbow. It may or may not have wings. When they are present, the wings are membranous. These are large ants, ranging from one-half to one inch long.

The ants are social insects and live in colonies numbering into the thousands. Carpenter ants tunnel into wood to build their homes, sometimes causing extensive damage to houses and other buildings. The best way to destroy a colony is by locating tunnel entrances and treating the tunnels and wood with poison placed in any sweet juice or fruit. If the problem persists, professional help should be sought.

Little Black Ant
page 111

Black to golden brown in color, this mostly wingless ant is more a nuisance than a serious pest. Its diet is anything humans eat, especially sweets, which is why it's sometimes called the sweet ant. Another name is the house ant. This small ant, about $1/16$ of an inch long, can be found day or night carrying food back to its colony, which is usually in the ground. Eliminating food sources is the best method of control, or you may use poisoned food available commercially. The similar Pharaoh ant in Florida and Louisiana can be a serious pest, chewing tunnels in the woodwork of houses.

Fire Ant
page 116

The fire ant, sometimes called the red ant, is found mainly in the southeastern United States, although its range seems to be expanding. Fire ants can be yellowish red to red in color and occasionally black. They are called fire ants because of their bite, not because of the way they look. Their bite produces a burning sensation because of the pinch and a chemical released. Fire ants have a large head and a very constricted waist with two segments, which means the abdomen is set further back than on other ants. The head has two huge jaws which of course are used to bite and produce the fiery sensation. The body, especially the thorax, has a fine hairlike covering over it which gives the ant a dull look as opposed to the shine of most other ants. Not a large ant, it is usually less than one-quarter inch long.

Voracious eaters, fire ants feed on insects, small frogs, and birds. Fire ants are able to kill these small animals by forging across the fields in battalions and attacking prey *en masse*. Using this method, they are able to prey upon animals hundreds of times larger than themselves. They will also eat many different plants, occasionally causing crop damage in gardens or in fields. Control of the ants is accomplished by digging up their nests and killing the ants or by using an insecticide. The nest, a series of chambers holding thousands of ants, eggs, and the queen, are normally underground, or sometimes in logs or rotting boards. Fire ants seem to be expanding their range northward. It is doubtful they will become prevalent too far north, however, because cold winters kill the colonies.

Termite
page 111

Termites are light-colored insects and are wingless, except for the kings and queens during swarming or mating. Termites are similar to ants except they don't have the narrow waist and their antennae are straight rather than bent. The soft body is nearly uniform in thickness from head to abdomen and is approximately one-quarter inch long. Termites have strong, chewing mouth parts and microorganisms in their stomachs to digest the wood they consume.

Termites live in colonies in the ground, so access to wood must be direct or through mud tunnels they construct. These will appear as thin mud tubes running from the ground up a masonry wall to wood beams. A metal barrier beneath the earth and the wooden frame of the structure will keep termites away from wood in buildings; preventive insecticides may also be used. Qualified exterminators will inspect homes for little or no charge. Away from our homes, termites are an asset because they clean up dead wood in the forest.

BEETLES

There are well over three hundred thousand species of beetles in the world, making up a good percentage of the total known animal population. Beetles are insects, and like all true insects have six legs and three body regions: the head, thorax or chest region, and abdomen. The head has compound eyes and antennae. The antennae often help identify different kinds of beetles. Beetles are characterized by their four wings. The two outer wings are hard and rigid, but the underwings are filmy and can fold up underneath the outer wings. Beetles have complete metamorphosis or four stages of development. The egg hatches into a larva (also called a worm or grub) which then feeds upon its host. It then pupates or goes into a resting stage and becomes an adult beetle.

For those who have gardens, beetles can be very annoying because they are probably the most voracious of the garden pests. Usually the stage of the beetle that is causing damage is either the larva or the adult. The leaf beetles are particularly damaging; in the leaf beetle group both the adults and the larvae feed upon leaves. They can be controlled by a number of methods. Check with your local garden center to determine which would be best for you.

Ladybird Beetle
page 114

Ladybird beetles, sometimes called ladybugs, are small, usually one-quarter inch long. They are round and stout with a very small thorax and head in comparison to the large wings and abdomen. They are generally orange or red with black spots. The larva of the ladybird beetle looks like a squat worm with its six legs located close to the front; the segmented abdomen often has hair on it. It is quite active and can move rapidly for a small caterpillar. The larva, although very tiny, can bite and cause some discomfort.

Most ladybird beetles are named by the number or the color of the spots on their backs such as a nine-spotted, a seven-spotted or a two-spotted ladybird beetle. Ladybird beetles are extremely beneficial insects to have both in the larval and the adult stages, because they eat other types of insects. They are particularly fond of aphids. Some nurseries and garden centers will sell you a supply of these beetles to put in your garden, especially if you do not want to use pesticides. Adult ladybirds gather together in huge numbers in autumn and migrate, spending the winter under rocks, branches, and leaves. If picked up, they often give off a disagreeable odor, causing most people to put them down again.

Firefly
page 113

Fireflies, also called lightning bugs in some parts of the United States, are not flies at all: they're beetles. The fireflies are about one-half inch in length and have a typical beetle shape although they are very slender. The shieldlike thorax, usually yellow to orangish yellow in color, covers the head. The black wings are usually bordered in yellow.

Like other beetles, fireflies go through complete metamorphosis. The eggs are laid under leaves or on rotted wood. The larvae or glowworms feed upon worms, snails, and other insects and grubs in the soil. The adults may feed on other insects, but many of them do not eat at all. The adults normally live or spend a lot of time in grassy fields, lawns, and trees. Fireflies are not serious garden pests.

We do not fully understood what causes the glowing light in the firefly and in some of the glowworms, but at dusk or after dark the soft yellowish white glow can be seen for hundreds of yards. Even some of the eggs can glow. Fireflies are a common summertime occurrence and add a mystique to the countryside, especially for children. Perhaps as we study the fireflies more we will learn how their cold light is produced and use this knowledge in our own production of light.

Click Beetle
page 113

The click beetle is so named because it is able to flip its thorax and abdomen and jump into the air; when it does this it makes a clicking sound. It has a special appendage between the thorax and abdomen that allows this to happen. Click beetles

flying
squirrel

fox
squirrel

red squirrel

thirteen-lined
ground squirrel

chipmunk

opossum

raccoon

spotted skunk

striped skunk

cottontail
rabbit

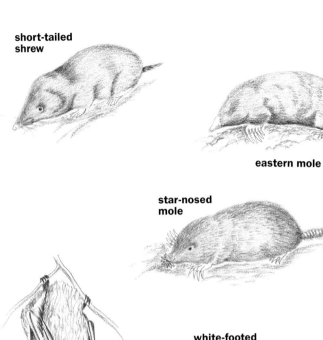

short-tailed shrew

eastern mole

star-nosed mole

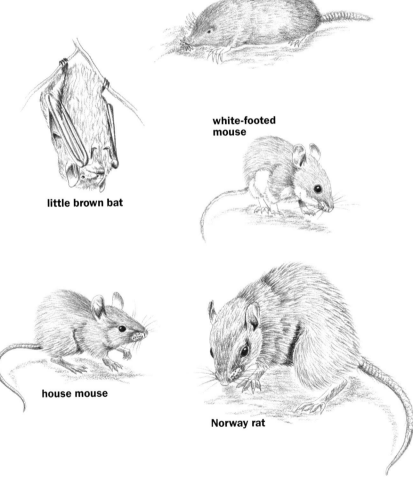

little brown bat

white-footed mouse

house mouse

Norway rat

red-tailed hawk

American kestrel

Cooper's hawk

Canada goose

turkey vulture

screech owl

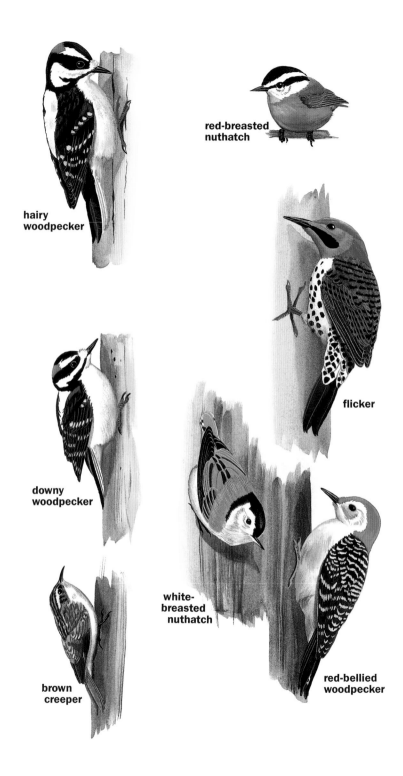

hairy
woodpecker

red-breasted
nuthatch

flicker

downy
woodpecker

white-
breasted
nuthatch

brown
creeper

red-bellied
woodpecker

male cardinal

female cardinal

male scarlet tanager

summer tanager

male house finch

male purple finch

male ruby-throated hummingbird

female scarlet tanager

house finch, yellow phase

yellow warbler

yellow-rumped warbler

magnolia warbler

evening grosbeak

American goldfinch

northern
oriole

American
redstart

robin

rufous-sided
towhee

nighthawk

chimney swift

tufted titmouse

dark-eyed junco

black-capped chickadee

Carolina chickadee

mockingbird

catbird

male indigo
bunting

blue jay

purple martin

barn swallow

bluebird

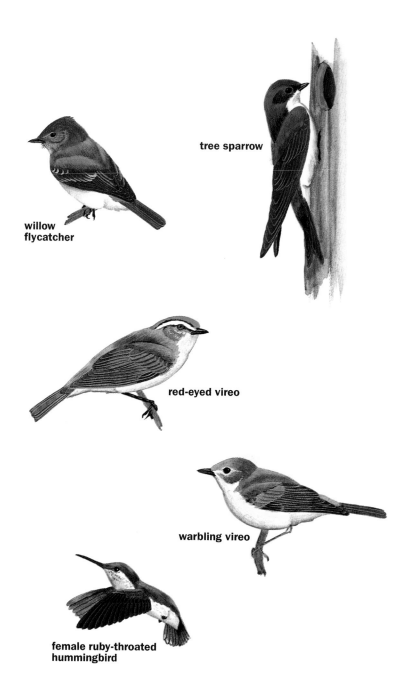

willow
flycatcher

tree sparrow

red-eyed vireo

warbling vireo

female ruby-throated
hummingbird

Bewick's wren

house wren

cedar waxwing

Carolina
wren

brown
thrasher

wood thrush

female indigo bunting

female cowbird

female house finch

female purple finch

mourning dove

white-crowned
sparrow

American tree
sparrow

chipping
sparrow

house sparrow

song
sparrow

fox sparrow

starling

male
cowbird

crow

red-winged
blackbird

common
grackle

five-lined skink

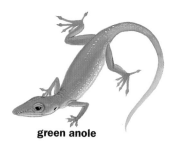

green anole

green tree frog

squirrel tree frog

greater grey tree frog

common toad

box turtle

southern toad

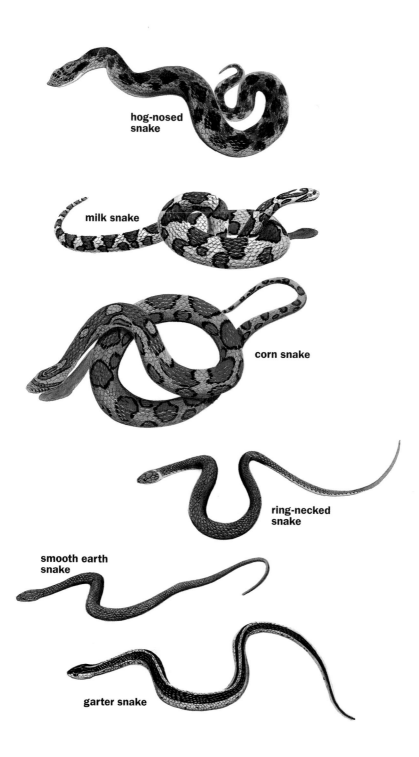

hog-nosed
snake

milk snake

corn snake

ring-necked
snake

smooth earth
snake

garter snake

centipede

millipede

pill bug

sow bug

white-lipped snail

striped forest snail

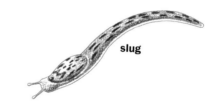

slug

earthworm

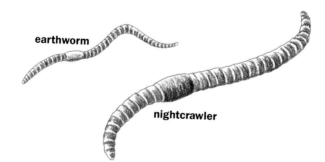

nightcrawler

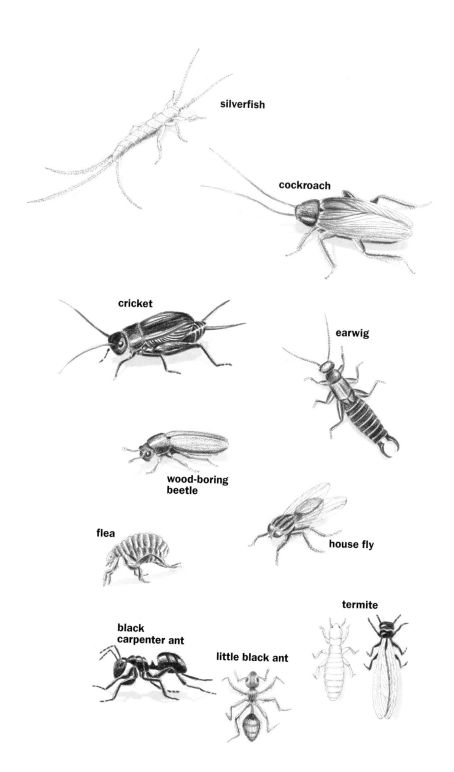

silverfish

cockroach

cricket

earwig

wood-boring beetle

flea

house fly

black carpenter ant

little black ant

termite

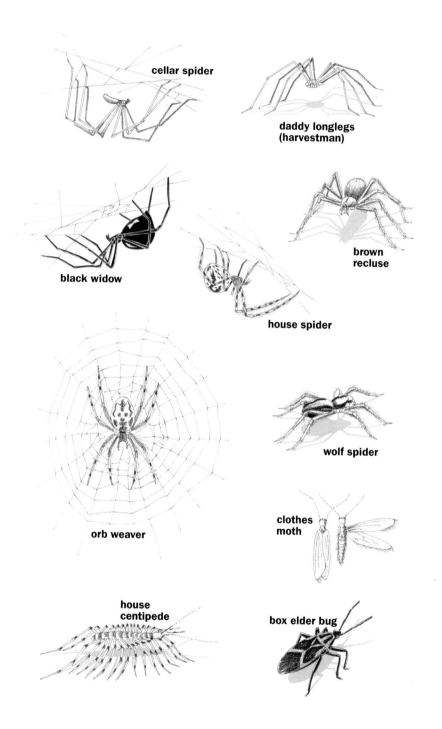

cellar spider

daddy longlegs
(harvestman)

black widow

brown
recluse

house spider

orb weaver

wolf spider

clothes
moth

house
centipede

box elder bug

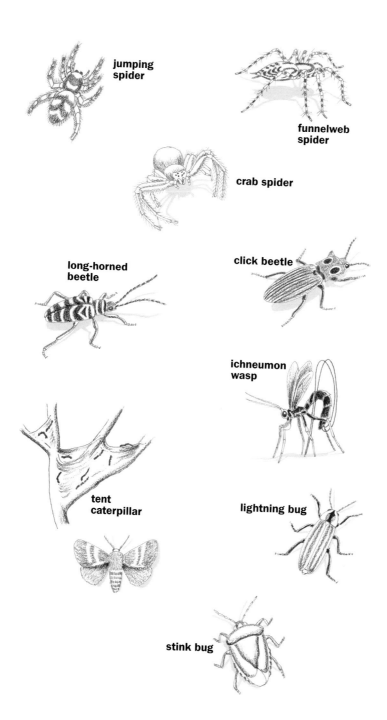

jumping spider

funnelweb spider

crab spider

long-horned beetle

click beetle

ichneumon wasp

tent caterpillar

lightning bug

stink bug

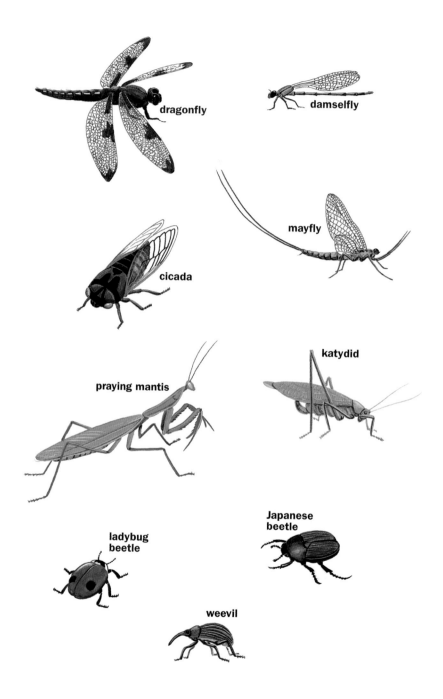

dragonfly

damselfly

mayfly

cicada

katydid

praying mantis

ladybug
beetle

Japanese
beetle

weevil

bean leaf
beetle

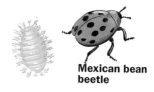
Mexican bean
beetle

striped cucumber
beetle

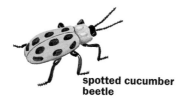
spotted cucumber
beetle

Colorado potato
beetle

striped blister
beetle

grasshopper

tomato
hornworm

cabbage
butterfly

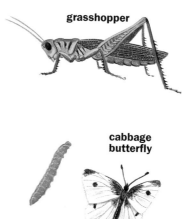

bald-faced hornet

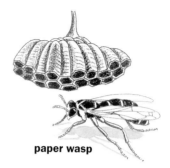

paper wasp

mud dauber wasp

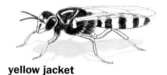

yellow jacket

bumblebee

honey bee

southern fire ant

horse fly

mosquito

tick

red admiral

great spangled fritillary

buckeye

eastern tailed blue

viceroy

monarch

common sulphur

American copper
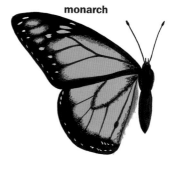

silver-spotted skipper

mourning cloak

pearl crescent

tiger swallowtail

black swallowtail

pipevine swallowtail

underwing

woolly bear moth

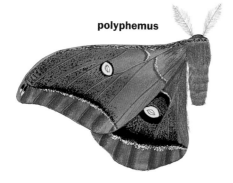

polyphemus

white-lined sphinx

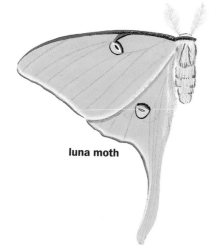

luna moth

rosy maple moth

royal walnut moth

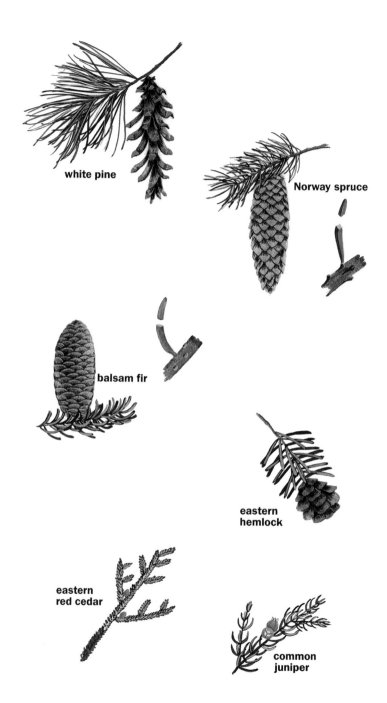

white pine

Norway spruce

balsam fir

eastern
hemlock

eastern
red cedar

common
juniper

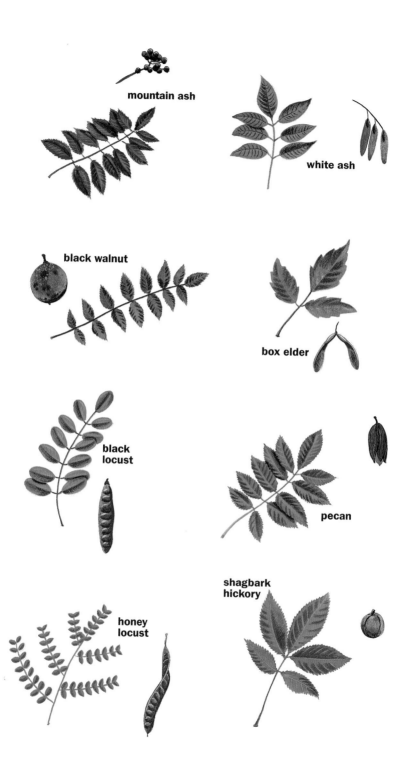

mountain ash

white ash

black walnut

box elder

black
locust

pecan

shagbark
hickory

honey
locust

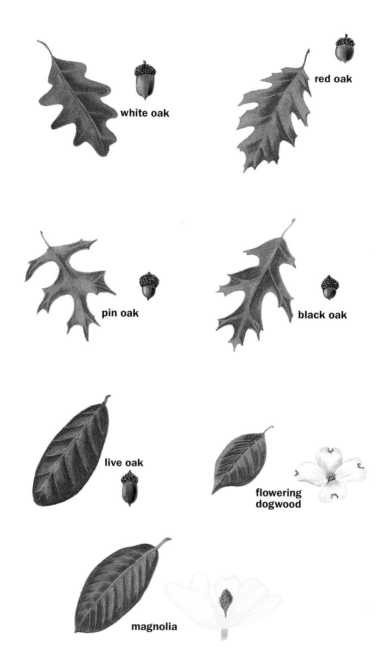

white oak

red oak

pin oak

black oak

live oak

flowering
dogwood

magnolia

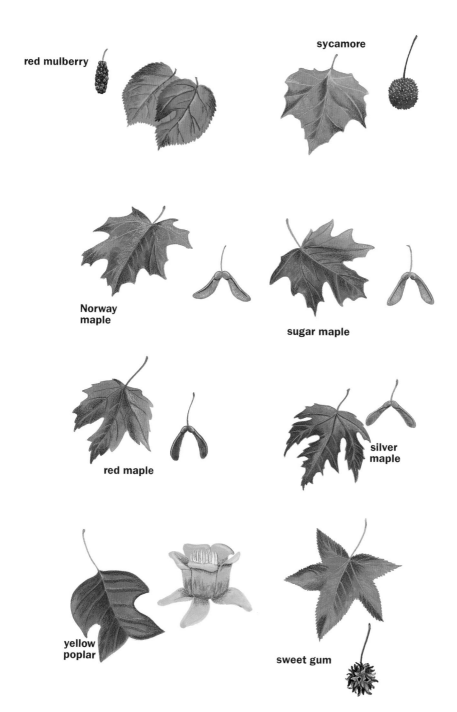

red mulberry

sycamore

Norway maple

sugar maple

red maple

silver maple

yellow poplar

sweet gum

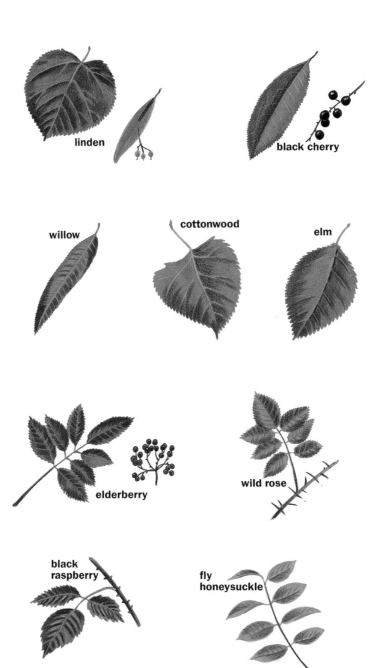

linden

black cherry

willow

cottonwood

elm

elderberry

wild rose

black raspberry

fly honeysuckle

bittersweet

trumpet vine

common
morning glory

jimsonweed

Japanese
honeysuckle

wild cucumber

kudzu

wild grape

Virginia
creeper

poison ivy

bittersweet
nightshade

black
nightshade

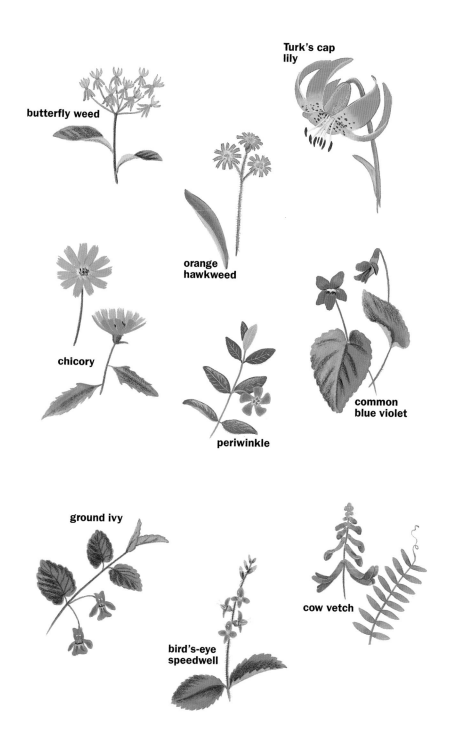

butterfly weed

Turk's cap lily

orange hawkweed

chicory

periwinkle

common blue violet

ground ivy

bird's-eye speedwell

cow vetch

celandine

St. Johnswort

purslane

buttercup

flower-of-an-hour

black mustard

sedum (wall pepper)

cinquefoil

yellow wood sorrel

bird's-foot trefoil

Virginia ground cherry

black-eyed Susan

dandelion

common tansy

yellow goatsbeard

yellow hawkweed

moth mullein

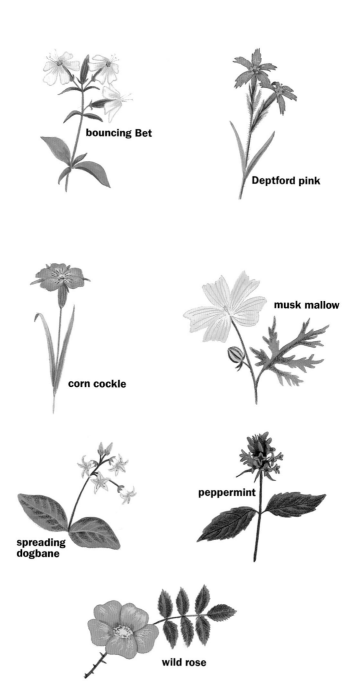

bouncing Bet

Deptford pink

corn cockle

musk mallow

spreading
dogbane

peppermint

wild rose

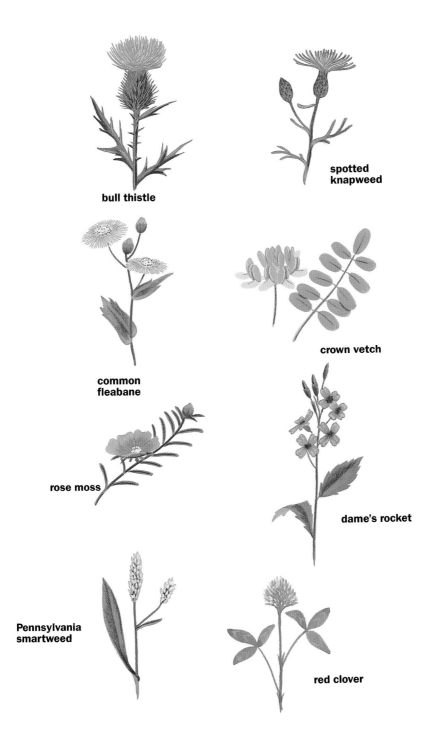

bull thistle

spotted
knapweed

common
fleabane

crown vetch

rose moss

dame's rocket

Pennsylvania
smartweed

red clover

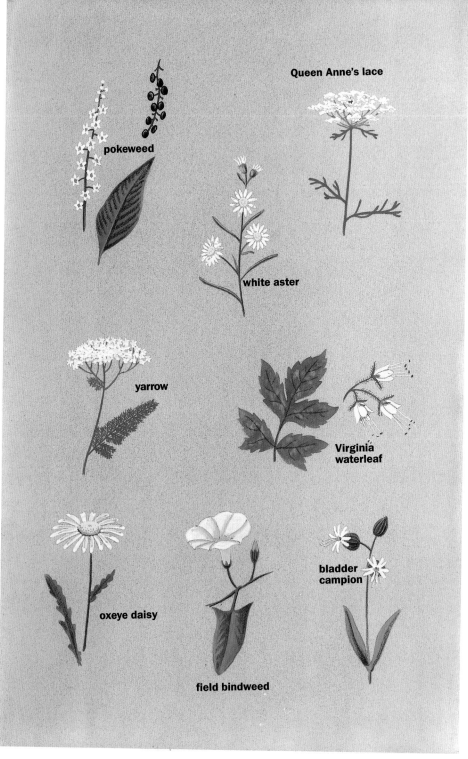

pokeweed

Queen Anne's lace

white aster

yarrow

Virginia waterleaf

oxeye daisy

field bindweed

bladder campion

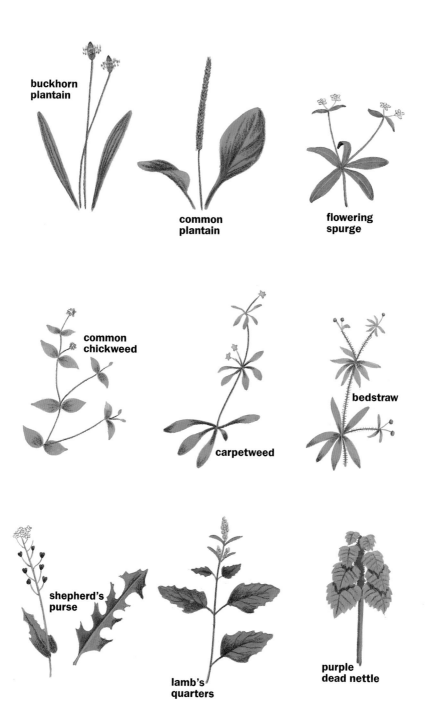

buckhorn plantain

common plantain

flowering spurge

common chickweed

carpetweed

bedstraw

shepherd's purse

lamb's quarters

purple dead nettle

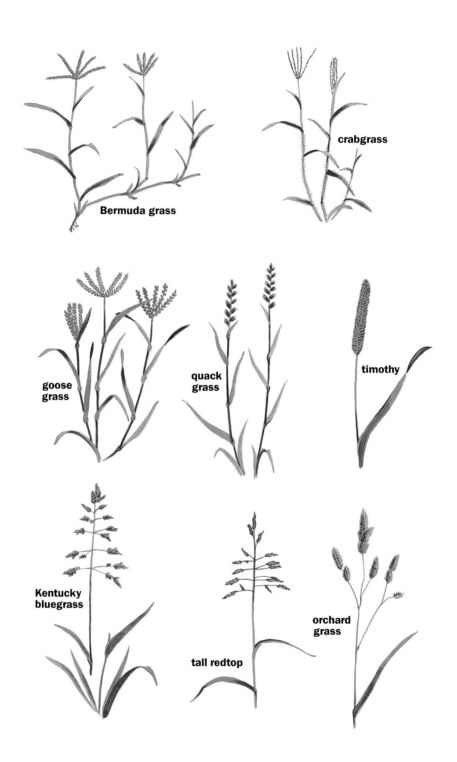

Bermuda grass

crabgrass

goose grass

quack grass

timothy

Kentucky bluegrass

tall redtop

orchard grass

bracken fern

Christmas fern

star moss

wall moss

silver moss

purple moss

**pixie cup
lichen**

**British
soldier**

shield lichen

**orange cup
fungus**

jelly fungus

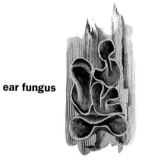

ear fungus

**common
liverwort**

**brown
stemonitis**

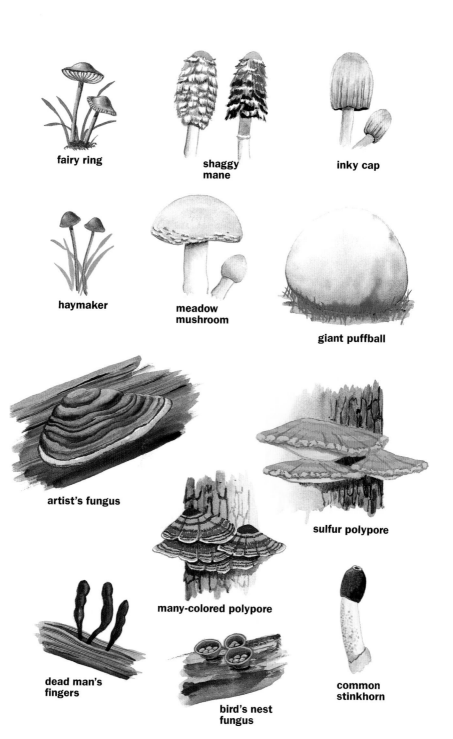

fairy ring

shaggy
mane

inky cap

haymaker

meadow
mushroom

giant puffball

artist's fungus

sulfur polypore

many-colored polypore

dead man's
fingers

bird's nest
fungus

common
stinkhorn

tray feeder

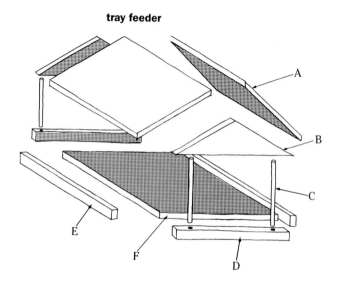

oriole feeder

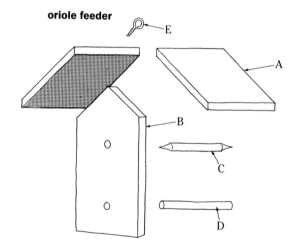

wren house

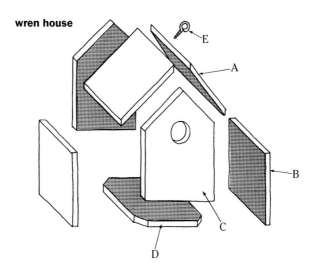

nesting roost

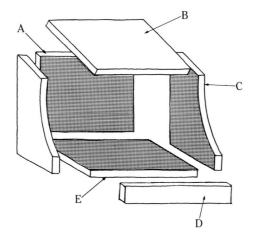

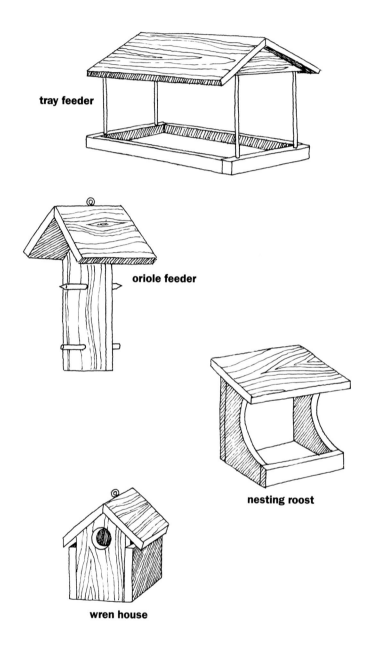

tray feeder

oriole feeder

nesting roost

wren house

are long, narrow beetles from $1/2$ to $1 1/2$ inches with long parallel stripes on the outer wings. Click beetles are usually gray, black, or brown in color. One species of click beetle has large black eye spots on the thorax. The body, besides being long and narrow, is also somewhat flat. The head is overshadowed by the prominent thorax.

The larvae of the click beetles are called wire worms. They are long, thin, and wiry and are dark brown or black. These worms feed on plant and animal material, especially dead trees, stumps, and rotten wood.

Sometimes click beetles cause damage to the trees and shrubs in our yards. Often the beetles spend the daytime hours underneath logs and leaves hidden from potential predators. If turned on its back, a click beetle will rest there for a second or two and then flip its thorax and abdomen, making the clicking noise, and hopefully land on its feet again. It keeps doing this until it rights itself. Some people think that the click beetle's flipping in the air unnerves predators and thus helps protect it.

June Bug

The June bug is not a bug at all, but a beetle. June bugs or June beetles (or May beetles, as some people call them) are about one inch long. They usually are dark brown to black in color, although one type of June beetle is green bordered with a little bit of brown or orange. The grubs are white, get fairly large, and live in the soil. They can grow up to about 1 to $1 1/2$ inches in length. The grubs eat the roots of different plants including grasses and shrubs.

The adults make lots of buzzing noises as they emerge from the ground, so they are easily picked up by young children and birds. They will not hurt anything, though they can be unnerving when they buzz furiously on the ground. Actually they are just trying to get into the air to fly away. They also have strong feet; a June bug crawling across your hand is quite a dramatic sensation.

June Bug,
continued

The green June beetle, which is predominately found in the south, can be a serious pest of fruits. The northern beetles usually eat only the leaves of plants. Occasionally an infestation of June beetles can cause some problems with lawns and gardens if there are too many of them. Treating the soil with an insecticide recommended by your local garden center or nursery is a good way to control them. Tilling is also effective because it kills the larvae in the soil.

June beetles are attracted to light during the summer so they will frequently be seen around street lights, porch lights, and on window and door screens. Since they are large, many night-foraging predators, including bats, whippoorwills, and nighthawks, may make use of them for food.

Potato Beetle

Potato beetles, both as larvae and as adults, feed upon the leaves of vegetable plants in our gardens. This beetle is green with long black stripes running the length of its wings and black stripes and dots on its thorax. Sometimes potato beetles can be quite numerous, the adults laying hundreds of eggs on the undersides of potato leaves, bean leaves, and other garden plants. They eat the softer parts of the leaves, and when they are finished the leaves are almost decimated; often only the harder veins are left.

If detected early enough the beetles can be picked off by hand and the leaves that carry eggs or young removed. For a large garden this is not practical, however, and some type of insecticide is necessary.

Colorado Potato Beetle
page 115

The Colorado potato beetle is from one-quarter to one-half inch long. It is quite a striking beetle: the wing covers have bright black and white or black and yellow stripes on them and the head and thorax are orange with black stripes.

This fairly round bug eats plants in the potato group including potatoes, tomatoes, eggplant, peppers, and cabbage. It can become quite abundant.

Colorado Potato Beetle, continued

The larva, a fat orange grub with black spots, attacks plants by eating the leaves. The eggs are orange and usually laid on the underside of a potato or tomato leaf. Fields nearby that have been used to raise some of these same types of plants will give these beetles a place to overwinter, so it is prudent to keep weed crops down to a minimum in fields near your garden. It is a relatively large beetle and also relatively slow. Therefore one of the best ways to control this insect in a small garden is to remove the larvae, egg masses, and adult beetles by hand.

Japanese Beetle
page 114

The Japanese beetle is one-half inch in size and can be found over the entire eastern United States. It feeds on many plants in our gardens, including fruit trees, shrubs, and some of our larger vegetables; it especially likes flowers. The adults have coppery brown wings that look somewhat metallic. The thorax is a metallic blue or green depending on how the light strikes it. The sides of the abdomen have white spots.

These beetles feed upon the soft parts of leaves, leaving behind a skeleton of the harder veins. This is called skeletonizing. The larvae, typical for beetles, are small white grubs that live in the ground and eat plant roots. This sometimes causes serious damage to lawns and shrubs as well as to older, larger plants. They can be controlled by insecticides and traps found at garden centers.

The grubs or larvae live in the soil for the first summer of their life and burrow deep below the frost line for the first winter. They then move upward and pupate. The adults emerge the second summer. This makes a two-year cycle. The Japanese beetle is probably an introduced species in the United States.

Spotted Cucumber Beetle
page 115

The spotted cucumber beetle is a narrow beetle, one-quarter to one-third inch long. The segmented antennae reach almost to the back of the body. The

Spotted Cucumber
Beetle,
continued

beetle's wings are green in color with black spots usually numbering eleven.

As the name indicates, the cucumber beetle feeds on the cucumber plant, but it will eat any plants that are vine-grown, such as squash, melons, and pumpkins. It is also a pest on some of the other plants in our garden such as potatoes and beans. The adults eat the whole leaf except for the very coarse veins which produces a haphazard, skeletonlike appearance. The beetles multiply throughout the summer, getting to be quite numerous. The adults overwinter in leaves and debris and lay their eggs in the springtime. The larvae feed upon roots of the same garden plants on which we find the adults.

Like all garden insects, cucumber beetles can transmit diseases from one plant to another and from one garden to another. One way to control the beetle is to plow your soil in the late fall after the insects have started to hibernate, thereby exposing them to the freezing elements; this keeps springtime breeding to a minimum. Because they are relatively small insects and also fairly quick fliers, control by hand picking is difficult.

Striped Cucumber Beetle
page 115

The striped cucumber beetle is another beetle that can cause serious damage to our vine crops. It is from one-quarter to one-third inch long and is a greenish yellow to yellow-orange in color with three black stripes on the back wings. The head is generally black.

The adults eat the leaves and flowers of the cucumber, causing serious damage especially to the new shoots. They have the same cycle as the spotted cucumber beetle, overwintering as adults with the larvae feeding on the roots of the host plants.

Bean Leaf Beetle
page 115

The bean leaf beetle is one-quarter inch long. It is an orangish yellow color with a black head, and black spots and stripes on the wings. As the name indicates, it feeds primarily on beans but also will feed on the pea family. The larva of the bean beetle is white and is found feeding upon the roots and nodules of the bean family plants.

Mexican Bean Beetle
page 115

The Mexican bean beetle is one that skeletonizes the bean plants. It is related to the ladybird beetle group and is a roundish beetle, one-third inch long, with a yellowish green body and black spots on the back. The thorax and head are also the yellowish green color. The yellow eggs are laid on the undersides of bean plants, usually in clusters. The larva is tiny, orangish green to yellowish green, and woolly, with spines on its thorax. It feeds on the undersides of leaves. The larvae do just as much damage to the bean leaves as do the adults. The adults overwinter by hibernating.

Striped Blister Beetle
page 115

The striped blister beetle is elongated instead of round and is one-half inch long. It is yellow and black striped including the head and thorax. The striped blister beetle feeds upon many of our vegetable plants including beans, beets, tomatoes, potatoes, and vinelike plants. The larvae of the blister beetles are beneficial, feeding on dirt insects or those found in the ground, especially grasshopper eggs. They can destroy an entire group of grasshopper eggs before they get big enough to hatch. In large enough numbers, the adult blister beetles can cause a problem for garden crops.

Weevil
page 114

Weevils are also called snout beetles because of their mouth parts. They are one-quarter to one inch long. A down-turned, long snout, sometimes very pronounced, is characteristic of this group of beetles. Weevils in most cases are a serious pest of crops. The curculio weevil is a predominant fruit pest. No mater what type of fruit crop you have there is some type of weevil that will cause problems with it.

Wood-boring Beetle
page 111

These metallic-colored beetles lay their eggs in dead and dying trees. The white larvae that cause the damage to wood are called flat-headed wood borers. Sometimes they may be found in household wood beams but most often enter the home with firewood.

The adults are long, from one-eighth to one inch, and have threadlike antenna. The hard shell-like forward wings cover up flying, fanlike wings underneath. This pretty beetle is not usually a serious household pest, but if it becomes one, professional extermination is required. Tiny holes in wood and small piles of wood powder are telltale signs.

Long-horned Beetle
page 113

Long-horned beetles are also called wood-boring beetles because the larval stage feeds on trees, boring into the bark or sometimes deep into the tree. The long-horned beetle can cause serious damage to the bark and the interior of the tree because they carry diseases such as Dutch elm disease. They range in size from three-quarters to one inch long and are recognized by their long antennae or horns. Sometimes these antennae can be two to three times as long as the body. Most long-horned beetles are a brownish color and some can be quite pretty; for instance, the locust borer is striped black and yellow and the elder borer is a blackish blue with a tan band across the beginning of the wings. All the long-horned beetles are long and tubular, looking somewhat like a bullet. Often the adult beetles feed on the nectar of flowers, especially the composites like the daisy.

One interesting adult long-horned beetle is the milkweed bug, or as some call it the red milkweed bug, a grayish red, slender beetle with long antennae. It feeds on the flowers of the milkweed. When picked up or irritated, milkweed bugs produce a "busy signal" sound. They make this noise by rubbing their wings together.

SPIDERS

Although spiders often conjure up a sinister picture, they are really quite interesting and in most cases quite harmless, with two exceptions. The only spiders in the United States that are dangerous are the black widow and brown recluse. Most other spiders have biting parts too small to pierce the skin of a human; those that can bite people usually only cause a small, itching bump.

Spiders in the home usually are not a problem, except that their webs collect dust, which annoys housekeepers. In fact, they can be quite beneficial because they feed mostly on insects. Spiders have two body parts (the cephalothorax and abdomen) and four pairs of legs. They eat by biting their prey; their teeth inject a poison that either kills or paralyzes it. Since spiders have few teeth, they liquefy the prey by injecting digestive liquids into it. Then they are able to suck out the juices, leaving only the empty exoskeleton. If they are unsuccessful in capturing anything they can go without food for several days. If they capture more food than they can eat right away, they wrap it in a cocoonlike layer of silk and save it for later.

One of the fascinating characteristics of most spiders is their ability to spin webs. The silk, which hardens upon contact with air, is one of the strongest fibers in nature. Scientists can identify the type of spider by its web design and placement and can even identify abnormal behavior by a different web design.

The spider's life cycle begins with mating. The male detects the presence of the female by the pheromones she gives off. Pheromones are chemical substances released into the air, much like the scent of perfume. The male can tell whether a female is receptive to mating by the feel of her web. Although the male is often smaller, the female is generally receptive. In many cases they share a web trap, the female at one end and the male at the other, until she is ready to mate. Some female spiders eat the males after mating, but this seldom occurs.

After a couple of weeks the female's eggs are mature and she lays an egg sac (or sacs) in a silk cocoon. The eggs may hatch in a few weeks or may overwinter. Because young spiders are apt to be a meal for a relative—or each other—many spin a long silk thread called a balloon into the air and allow themselves to be carried away in the wind. A field of ballooning spiders is called a gossamer. Autumn is a good time to watch for these ballooning young spiders.

As a spider's body grows it must leave its exoskeleton and manufacture a new one. Spiders normally live one or two seasons, although tarantulas and their relatives can live up to twenty years in captivity.

In the same general group as spiders (arachnids), we find chiggers, ticks, and harvestmen, sometimes called daddy longlegs. All these creatures have the same basic body makeup and share a common ancestry.

House Spider, Cellar Spider, or Cobweb Spider
page 112

The house spider (also called cellar spider or cobweb spider) is probably the most common spider we come across in our homes. A little more than one-quarter inch long, it is medium to dark brown with black lines running across the legs and along the body, making a circular target effect on the sides. The abdomen is extremely large in comparison to the rest of the spider. It is also called the comb-footed spider because of the comblike apparatus on the legs.

The cobweb spider likes to hide in the corners of rooms and under furniture. It comes out at night and produces webs under the furniture and in the corners of windows and ceilings. The webs have no particular shape. When an insect gets entangled in its web, the spider encircles or wraps it in a layer of silk and injects it with poison. Later it sucks out the body liquids and allows the carcass to drop to the ground.

The name cobweb comes from old grist mills where the webs were formed in corners. Being sticky, they caught the dust produced when the corn was removed from the cobs. Not a very fast spider, it is easily controlled with a broom or dust mop.

Orb Weaver Spiders
page 112

The orb weavers are a large group of outdoor spiders that make webs we call orbs. They can vary dramatically in color and size, measuring anywhere from $1/16$ inches to over 1 inch long; the males are generally the smaller of the two. Although orb weavers are often typical cylindrical brown spiders, they can be quite interesting in appearance: black, yellow, mahogany, white, or any combination of these colors. They sometimes have a huge fat body with many striking markings on it. These markings range from whites and blacks to oranges and yellows. A few orb weavers have very striking body shapes; some resemble thorns or shields and others are somewhat crab-shaped.

The orb weaver most commonly found in our gardens is the yellow argiope or black and yellow argiope. It has striking yellow and black markings on the body. Occasionally you may find the shamrock and marbled spiders, which have roundish bodies with orange, white, and black markings on them. They are very pretty spiders. Another group of orb weavers are those that have hard shells and spines, much like a hermit crab or horseshoe crab. These may have dramatically different shapes and colorations.

The orb weaver makes a web in a spiral shape, hence the name orb. It usually puts out support lines first; once the support lines are completed, the spider spins in an oval or circular pattern. The male will often make another smaller orb near the female's or even take over her orb if she is willing. Orb weaver spiders usually spin their orbs between different plants. They place the webs across paths that insects might fly or crawl along. They thereby capture many insects during the day and in the evening. The spiders often produce a new web every night, taking approximately an hour to complete it.

An orb weaver has very poor eyesight, so it must capture its prey by sensing motion on the web. It hides off to one side of the orb until an insect gets entangled in the web. Once this happens the spider rushes out, poisons the insect with a bite, and wraps it in silk. It will then take the package to the center of the web or carry it off to the side. If an object other than an insect should happen to get caught in the web, the spider cuts it out and repairs the web.

Jumping Spider
page 113

Jumping spiders are spiders that pounce on their prey. They have also been called fly spiders because of their habit of jumping on and capturing flies. Jumping spiders are one-quarter to one-half inch long and are predominantly brown or black with varied markings on their backs. These markings are sometimes very colorful, intricate patterns of browns, yellows, and oranges. Jumping spiders are relatively squat and have lots of hair on their bodies. Their eyes are large, giving them a menacing look.

A jumping spider rarely makes a web, but occasionally will use a type of web as a safety line on which it can crawl back after a jump. It spins these filaments from a crevice or small space to hide in, especially during the night. The eyesight of a jumping spider is extremely good; it can identify insect prey a foot away. The jumping spider can be found both inside and outside. Its favorite spots outdoors are alongside buildings, on rocks, and on plants.

Funnelweb Spider
page 113

Funnelweb spiders are the same size as jumping spiders, one-quarter to one-half inch long, and are easily identified. They are brown or sometimes gray-brown, and their abdomen has two long spinnerets, often half the length of the abdomen, through which their silk comes for the webs. The thorax is very shiny and shieldlike and the eyes are set in the forward portion of the thorax. The spider has a large *chelicera*, jaws that contain teeth.

The webs of these spiders are spun at the edges of plants and roots, at the bases of rocks, in the corners of buildings, anywhere there is a natural crevice in which the spider can hide. In the early mornings when the dews are heavy it is easy to spot the webs with their droplets of water. At one end of the web is a tube or funnel where the spider conceals itself.

Black Widow Spider
page 112

This spider is about one-half inch long. It is a beautiful jet black and the underside of the abdomen sports an orange or bright red hourglass shape. Because the female is notorious for its poisonous bites, the black widow is a spider you need to be aware of, although the bite is not necessarily fatal.

The black widow was more commonly encountered when people spent more time outdoors in their normal daily routines, such as using an outdoor toilet or harvesting most of their food by hand. Because of changing lifestyles, the bite of the black widow spider is not experienced much today. Nevertheless, you should take care whenever you are in your yard, in the countryside picking berries, or moving around outbuildings, dumps, or campsites. The best way to avoid this spider is to keep your body, especially your hands, out of places that you cannot see into.

Again, the bite is not necessarily fatal, but it can cause severe problems. The black widow may not even hurt when it first bites you. The pain usually comes from the secondary effects of the poison. You may get a pain in your stomach, in your muscles, or in your joints. You then may experience symptoms similar to those of rabies: your saliva starts to flow, your mouth feels dry, and you experience hot flashes, sweating, and an all-over miserable feeling. Doctors can treat the poison either with injections that relieve the symptoms or with anti-venom.

The black widow spider does spin a web, so always be aware of spider webs. The male spider, which is smaller and has longer legs, does not bite and does not use a web.

Brown Recluse Spider
page 112

The brown recluse is another spider whose bite can be dangerous to man. It is brown all over with a lighter brown thorax. The brown recluse is also sometimes called the violin spider because it has a light orange mark somewhat the shape of a violin on the top of the thorax. It is normally less than one-half inch long.

This is an indoor spider that commonly hides behind furniture, beneath chairs, and under beds, and sometimes gets into clothing and shoes. Though not really an aggressive spider, it is quite secretive, so when it is disturbed or trapped it bites instinctively for defense. Often the bite of this spider is not noticed. It causes a bit of swelling and a crust forms on the bite. This can become quite enlarged and the wound can take a long while, sometimes months, to heal. As with most spider bites, the tissue around the bite usually disintegrates and dies, causing a permanent deformity.

The brown recluse does not spin a web; it runs to capture its prey and eats the victim right away. It is for the most part a southern spider and is not found very often in northern parts of North America. If you are in an area that brown recluses are known to inhabit, it is best to shake clothing and shoes before putting them on, especially if they have been lying on the floor.

Crab Spider
page 113

Crab spiders, as their name indicates, are shaped like crabs. Their legs come out from the sides of the body and are very long and bent forward like crab pincers. Frequently the thorax and abdomen have brightly colored protuberances similar to those of crabs. Many crab spiders are colored brilliantly to mimic the plants they hide on, especially the yellows, reds, tans, and browns of flowers. They are only about one-quarter inch long.

Crab spiders are predacious; they do not capture their food by spinning webs. Instead they wait in ambush underneath flower heads and run sideways, again reminiscent of the crab, to grab insects and other prey. Many people call them flower spiders because they sit on the tops of flowers and are not easily noticed unless disturbed. Then they scuttle quickly sideways or backward.

Wolf Spider
page 112

Wolf spiders are found just about everywhere; most often we find them close to the ground looking for something to eat. They are brown to gray-brown in color. The wolf spider has eight eyes, four small ones in a row and four larger ones above. Most wolf spiders are under one-half inch long, usually under one-third of an inch. They have relatively long legs, usually about two-thirds of the entire body length.

Wolf spiders do not normally spin webs. Most are nocturnal and feed at night in the summertime, although during the cold season they may feed during the daytime. The female carries the brown, papery egg sac on her back for a few weeks. The young (usually about twenty) stay with the female for a short time and then disperse.

Wolf spiders are often kept as pets. They are interesting to watch as they stalk their prey. They need places to hide, a constant source of food—any type of insect will do—and water in a container. Although not poisonous, wolf spiders can bite, and some people have had minor reactions to them. As with any spider, it's best to take precautions.

Harvestman or Daddy Longlegs
page 112

Daddy longlegs or harvestmen are not true spiders but are related to them. They have a broadly fused cephalothorax and extremely long legs. They can be anywhere from black to light brown in color. Their bodies are one-quarter to one-half inch long; with the legs added some are almost three inches in length. These long legs allow the body to hang close to the ground with the middle joints of the legs very high. If grabbed by one of its legs a daddy longlegs can easily pull loose, leaving the leg behind.

Daddy longlegs do not spin webs. Feeding mainly at night, they eat insects, mites, and other little creatures. They have a spraying stink gland they can activate if picked up. The eggs are laid in the ground. Harvestmen may overwinter under a log or in the forest floor litter, but in the northern part of the country most adults will freeze and only the eggs will produce daddy longlegs for the following year.

Chigger

Chigger is a general name for a number of nearly microscopic mites that attack animals. All that is visible to the naked eye is a red dot. They are related to the spiders, having a round body with eight legs.

Chiggers are parasitic upon mammals. They can be serious pests of pets, causing scab and mange. On humans they are more of an irritation; they dig into the skin and cause a reaction that itches dramatically. Insect repellent is the best control for parts of the body where chiggers may come into contact with you. They lie in wait for prey in grasses and low-lying foliage, so repellent used below the knees is usually sufficient. Because chiggers can carry disease, such as skin disease and typhus, prevention is a good practice to follow.

Chiggers seem to be more common in the southern part of the eastern United States than in the northern part. Because of their small size, they are most easily recognized by the characteristic bite they give. Usually these bites appear near where clothing is constricting to the body, such as at your waist or at cuffs or at the brief line on your underclothing, because chiggers burrow into the skin where the clothing prevents them from crawling further. After feeding, they fall off.

Tick
page 116

The tick is a relative of the spider family with four pairs of legs. Normally ticks are less than one-quarter inch long. They are generally flat-bodied and have very small heads. Ticks are dark brown with different markings on them. They sometimes have stripes, sometimes dots, and sometimes just irregular patterns. Male ticks are usually more brightly patterned than females.

Ticks are parasites and feed mostly on the blood of mammals. The female tick grasps onto the clothing or hair of a mammal, climbs up, attaches itself to the skin, and sucks a meal of blood. Sometimes it drinks so much it becomes bloated and appears grayish. Once it has its fill, it will drop off and lay eggs to begin a new cycle. The eggs are laid in leaf litter or in a secluded area. When the larvae hatch they immediately crawl up some kind of vegetation and attach themselves to a host, often remaining until they are adults.

The tick usually lies in the grass and waits for a host to come by. It stretches its legs out and if something brushes against it, it grabs hold. Ticks are usually host specific: they will attach themselves to only one type of mammal or group of mammals. They are able to tell by the pheromones and ammonia given off by the body of a mammal whether it is the right one. Parts of the life cycles of ticks may require them to feed upon a different host such as mice, rabbits, and squirrels. Sometimes they may even attach onto another tick for a short period.

The most common ticks that we see in the eastern United States are the wood ticks and dog ticks. Both of these are fairly common in old fields and forest edges and in our backyards. Deer ticks are also widespread; they are smaller than other ticks and their bodies are reddish brown with a black spot on the head.

Ticks can carry diseases. Two diseases that are causing some concern are Rocky Mountain Spotted Fever, not very often found in the eastern United States, and Lyme Disease, which is becoming more prevalent. Checking your body and your pets for ticks after being out in the field is a good method of keeping tick infestations to a minimum. Protect pets with sprays or collars; insect repellents with DEET

Tick,
continued

in them work on human clothing and skin. Spray the repellent on your clothing around your ankles and around places where you brush against the grass. These same repellents will work for mosquitoes, fleas, and chiggers.

To remove a tick that has already dug into the skin, place tweezers very close to the front of the tick, right by its mouth, and gently tug backwards. It is best not to squeeze the abdomen because this forces juices onto your skin. If you have been bitten by a tick in an area where a disease is prevalent, it is best to seek medical attention.

Since ticks are hardy critters, there are only a few sure ways of killing them easily. One is to squash them between two hard objects, such as rocks; the other is to burn them with a match.

BEES AND WASPS

Bees and wasps belong to the group called *hymenoptera*. They have the general insect characteristics of six legs and three body parts. They usually have four wings that are membranous or translucent. A difference between bees and wasps is that bees generally have hairy bodies whereas wasps have smooth bodies. Both usually have chewing mouth parts that they use to chew their food whether it be an animal, pollen, or nectar. They have modified ovipositors—egg-laying appendages—located on the abdomen. These ovipositors can be used to sting, causing quite a lot of pain in certain instances. They are also used to paralyze prey that will be fed to the larvae.

Bees and wasps have complete metamorphosis with egg, larval, pupal, and adult stages. Many of the bees and wasps are communal and have a caste system of drones, workers, and queens. The workers are females that are not fertilized; the drones are males that have no other purpose than to mate with the queen; and the queen of course lays the eggs. The caste system is very complex and may number from a few individuals up to thousands as in the honey bees. Most hymenoptera are quite beneficial, although with their ability to sting they can cause great discomfort and even death. Bees and wasps are normally attracted to our yards because of the flowers that we plant and the protection found in our trees and shrubs where they often build their nests. The nests can also be in the ground, in rock walls, or most anyplace a hole or opening is located.

Bald-faced Hornet
page 116

Like all bees and wasps, the bald-faced hornet has a narrow waist where the body constricts between the thorax and the abdomen. This feature helps tell the difference between bees and other insects. Bees and wasps have four filmy wings. The bald-faced hornet has black and white blotches on its face, giving it the name bald-faced or white-faced. Sometimes these blotches can be yellow. The body is predominately black with some yellow or whitish parts on it. Semi-transparent instead of clear, the wings are a dark gray color. Our largest wasp, at least in body size, at one-half to three-quarters inches, the bald-faced hornet can be a serious pest if the nest is disturbed.

The mated queen emerges from the ground in springtime. She chews bark and dead plant material into a paperlike substance from which she makes a new nest, usually hanging it in the open from a tree branch. The female lays a few eggs in this small walnut-sized nest and takes care of the larvae as they mature and emerge from the pupae stage. These newly hatched hornets then help the female build a larger nest where she lays an additional forty or fifty eggs; they also help her to take care of the new larvae, feeding them chewed-up insect parts. When these have matured, they then can build a larger nest and so the summer progresses with the nest being repeatedly torn apart and made larger until by the end of the summertime, hundreds of young hornets can be emerging weekly. Fall is when the bald-faced hornets are usually noticed because they are present in the largest numbers. During the fall, young males and unmated females will mate. These mated females will then burrow into the ground to overwinter. The rest of the colony dies and these mated females are the only ones to emerge the next spring.

It is best to leave the nests alone until you are sure the fall frosts have taken their toll. Once frost

Bald-faced Hornet, continued

has killed the entire colony, the nest can be taken down and used as a showcase or a decoration for the home or backyard. Bald-faced hornets are extremely aggressive if you damage their nest. When they find an enemy they sting, emitting a pheromone that attracts the rest of the nest to battle. Unlike honeybees, hornets can sting repeatedly and can cause severe pain. If you wish to remove the nest, it is best done at night when all the hornets are in it. One of the best methods is to place the nest in a huge garbage bag filled with insecticide. Occasionally, like the yellow jackets, the bald-faced hornets may place their nest in a hole underground. The nests are made of pancake-shaped layers of egg and larva chambers.

Yellow Jacket
page 116

The body of the yellow jacket is fat and stout, much like the bald-faced hornet's but usually smaller. The body is black and yellow from the thorax back over the abdomen, hence the name yellow jacket. The wings are a dusky brown color and semi-transparent.

Like the bald-faced hornet, the adult eats nectar and other insects and feeds its larvae chewed-up insects. The yellow jacket is not intimidated by humans; it often feeds at picnic tables and will actually fly away with meat scraps and other delectables. If disturbed it can sting quite aggressively, especially near the nest. The nest is paper-like and is built similarly to the bald-faced hornet's, starting with a small walnut-sized nest and growing larger as the colony gets bigger. Yellow jackets also can nest underground, in hollow logs, or in any crevice. For that reason their nest is more difficult to detect than a hornet's nest. If you start seeing a number of yellow jackets around your yard, watch where they go. If you can find the nest, removing it at night or using a commercial hornet and wasp spray is best.

Young females mate in the fall; these fertilized females are the only ones to live through the winter,

Yellow Jacket,
continued

hiding under logs, plant litter, and debris. As spring approaches, they emerge and each start a new colony. In areas of severe winters, even these female yellow jackets will not all survive and so the colonies are fewer. On the other hand, when we have a very mild winter, there will be a great abundance of yellow jackets by the end of the summer. Like the hornet nest, the yellow jacket nest is made up of layers of egg and larva chambers.

Paper Wasps
page 116

Paper wasps are usually from one-half to over three-quarters inches long. They can vary in color but are normally some shade of brown to reddish brown; they sometimes have black and yellow stripes across the thorax and abdomen. They are found all over the eastern United States. In the south the wasp with yellow stripes dominates; the northern paper wasp is almost devoid of striping.

These wasps make nests in an inverted umbrella shape descending from a stalk. They chew leaves and other cellulose material to produce a paperlike substance. The nest is usually hung in a protected place under the eaves of houses, inside garages, or wherever the nest will be sheltered from the weather. Unlike the nests of hornets and yellow jackets, the paper wasp nest is not covered on the outside with a cocoonlike shell. The nest contains from five to thirty egg-laying chambers where the females deposit the eggs. Both adults feed these larvae nectar, pollen, and insects until they pupate, usually in a few weeks.

Paper wasps are normally quite docile, not causing problems for humans unless they are disturbed. When they are agitated, however, they can sting a number of times. If you wish to remove the nest, the best time to do it is at night either by smashing it with a mallet or using wasp spray.

Newly mated females overwinter in crevices or cracks in the ground or around the house, sometimes between the windows, so you might notice them coming into the house in early spring.

Mud Dauber Wasp
page 116

These wasps can be anywhere from one-quarter to three-quarters of an inch long. Slim in appearance, they have very narrow, constricted abdomens at the front that get wider towards the end of the insect. The transparent wings can have a bluish to grayish cast. The body is usually black or blue-black. Some have yellow spots on them. Adult mud daubers feed mainly on spiders and insects.

All mud daubers are characterized by their mud-collecting habits and mud nests. Each species makes a very particular type of nest. A common shape is four or five vertical tunnels constructed against a flat surface. The female collects a mouthful of mud and then places it in concentric circles in columns sometimes shaped like organ pipes. In these nests, the eggs are laid. Whatever the wasp preys upon will also be placed inside so that as the eggs hatch, the larvae have something to eat. The nests are built one chamber at a time. Once the female has laid an egg and placed the prey inside the cell, she then seals the mud chamber and starts a new cell. After the larva hatches and eats the intended prey, it will pupate and emerge from the mud chamber.

Mud daubers can be found lots of different places. Some of their tunnels can be found on the sides of houses, under the eaves, or on trees and cement blocks nearby. Generally a solitary builder of mud chambers, the mud wasp is not aggressive unless you disturb the nest. Occasionally woodpeckers may find these chambers, peck them open and eat the larvae inside.

There is a parasite of the mud dauber called the cuckoo wasp. It lays its eggs in the mud dauber's chamber before it is completed, which allows the hatched cuckoo wasp larvae to feed on the prey intended for the mud dauber larvae; when this happens the mud dauber young often starve.

Ichneumon Wasp
page 113

The ichneumon wasp, or ichneumon fly, ranges from $1/16$ inch to over 2 inches long. The wings are a transparent smoky color and the body can be brown, black or gray. The most conspicuous feature on ichneumons is the extremely long ovipositor, or egg-laying appendage, on the female; it is sometimes five times as long as the entire body. The females use the ovipositors to lay eggs on other insects or on trees where insects are found. The eggs are parasitic to the host they are laid upon.

Ichneumon wasps were brought to the United States to control beetles found in cereal and other crops. They do provide extensive help with controlling insect pests in our gardens, such as the tomato horn worm. Ichneumons usually do not sting humans. Like all wasps, they are beneficial to have around as long as they don't interfere with humans—or rather, as long as humans don't interfere with them.

Bumble Bee
page 116

Bees are a little different from wasps. They normally have pollen baskets on their hind legs that they use to collect pollen, which they take back to eat. Bees also have lots of body hair. The bumble bee is a large fat bee from one-half to one inch long. It is black with varying bands of yellow; sometimes it is almost all black and sometimes almost all yellow. The bumble bee has a long mouth part called a tongue that allows it to reach deep into flowers such as clover and composite flowers such as daisies for the nectar. The wings are a translucent blackish gray, sometimes almost brown.

Bumble bees nest in holes in the ground, often taking over abandoned mouse nests or chipmunk nests. Young female bumble bees mate in the fall, then hibernate underground over the winter. They

Bumble Bee, continued

emerge in the springtime to lay eggs and begin new colonies. The fertilized females are the only ones that live through the winter. Bumble bees are not exceptionally fast fliers, and they fly erratically looking for pollen from different plants. Bumble bees are not normally aggressive and do not bother people unless you happen to step on them or their ground nest. These nests are flat, layered chambers similar to those of the paper wasp.

Honey Bee
page 116

Honey bees are typical bees with hairy bodies and translucent smoky-colored wings. They are a dark brown to black with alternate bands of tan or brownish yellow from the thorax all the way along the abdomen. They are about one-half inch long.

Honey bees are probably one of the best known insects, mainly because they are very beneficial, pollinating lots of plants for us including all our fruit and vegetable crops. They also provide us with wax and honey.

Honey bees can be found at almost all flowers in our yards any time that they are blooming. They often frequent bird feeders if there is corn meal dust present, especially early in the spring when food supplies may be sparse. They also like the nectar found in hummingbird feeders and will visit the edges of our birdbaths to get water during hot, dry summer days. Honey bees are colonial insects and live in hives. Besides man-made commercial hives the colonies also can be found in hollow trees, in corners of buildings, and under eaves. The hive normally contains a queen (a fertile female), workers (nonfertile females) and drones (males). The workers and the drones take care of the queen and the eggs. The workers, as their name implies, are the ones who do most of the work. They leave the hive to gather nectar and pollen and feed the larvae in the cells. Both workers and drones live only a few weeks to perhaps two months during the summertime.

Honey bees are dependent upon flowers and nectar sources. They have a method of communication among themselves called a tailwag dance. By doing this dance the bee can tell other bees where sources of nectar and pollen are, how far away they are, and in what direction they are located. Honey bees store nectar in the form of honey in the hive. It is used to feed the hive during winter. They overwinter as adults feeding upon the honey. To keep themselves warm, they make a huge living ball of bees with the queen normally inside. Occasionally after a long or stressful winter, bees in commercial hives have to be fed additional food during the springtime.

When a hive grows too large, a second queen will be allowed to live and will eventually leave, taking a portion of the bees with her. This is called swarming. This group then creates a new hive where the young queen mates and begins laying eggs.

Honey bees can be found all over the eastern United States although in the extreme far north they are not quite as plentiful because they cannot survive the long winters.

BUTTERFLIES

Over ten thousand species of butterflies can be found in North America. Butterflies are in a group called *lepidoptera*, meaning scaled wings. These scales produce their bright colors. Handling butterflies will remove these scales and cause them to have difficulty flying, so it is best not to touch them. Although the caterpillars can be striking in coloration, little discussion will be focused on them unless they are extremely noteworthy.

Butterflies have two pairs of wings attached to the first and second part of the thorax. Like all insects, they have three body parts: the head, the thorax, and the abdomen. The legs and wings are attached to the thorax or chestlike region. Butterflies have long antennae, which are sometimes club-shaped on the end and can be of help in identification. A long, coiled proboscis extends from the mouth. They use this to sip nectar from flowers.

All butterflies go through a complete metamorphosis. They lay their eggs on a host plant and the eggs hatch into caterpillars or worms. The caterpillars then go into a resting stage, becoming pupae and forming a chrysalis. The chrysalis is a hard case made from the inside of the caterpillar's skin. Sometimes it can be quite brightly colored and has very definite shapes which can help identify the type of caterpillar. Some types of butterflies and moths spin a cocoon. Their silk glands produce silk which they spin into a web around themselves, creating a small capsule. They pupate inside of this. If the caterpillar happens to have hair it may also incorporate the hair into this cocoon. The life span of butterflies and moths can vary from a short period of a month or less to over a year.

The most destructive phase in both butterflies and moths is usually the caterpillar stage. These are the insects that frequently damage plants and animals because of their voracious eating habits. The adults are usually harmless; they are generally nectar eaters, feeding upon flowers and nectar-bearing plants. Often they do not even eat during their life span but concentrate solely on producing eggs. Butterflies can overwinter in all four stages: egg, pupa, larva, and adult. The overwintering stage determines when the adults will emerge and mate. They can mate in the fall, during the early spring, and during the summer. They may have more than one brood per year, which also determines when they mate.

Butterflies are one of the most numerous and noticeable insects in our yards. Because they fly slowly and are strikingly colored, they are fun to entice and watch. Many people grow flowers and plants that attract the butterflies and their larvae.

Butterflies may be observed closely during the evening by attracting them to a light. This method also attracts moths. Nectar is another means of luring the butterflies in for a closer look. Butterflies can be reared in captivity by collecting the eggs or larvae from the host plants.

Since certain species can be endangered almost to extinction by collectors, butterfly collections are now frowned upon. It is illegal in some cases to collect certain species. There are now groups of people that are called butterfly watchers who watch and study butterflies but do not collect them. Planting flowers for butterflies is a popular way to watch them. Besides cultivating the flowers needed to attract the colorful adult butterfly, it is also beneficial to grow the food plants necessary for the larva. Many garden centers and nurseries specialize in plants for butterflies.

Great Spangled Fritillary
page 117

The fritillary is called the brush-footed butterfly because of its small forelegs. The forelegs are the two legs found at the front that are covered with hair, and they are so small the butterfly cannot use them for walking. Fritillaries range from 3¹/₂ to 4 inches at the widest part of the wing. They are a striking orangish brown overall with black and brown lines across the wings and along the wing edges. The underside of their wings is a lighter orange and they have very pronounced silver spots. Probably the most notable characteristic of fritillaries is their habit of folding their wings up over their backs.

Larvae of the great spangled fritillary feed mainly on violets. The fritillaries will visit most any meadow flower during the summertime. They are probably the largest group of butterflies that we see in our backyards.

Monarch
page 117

The monarch is probably the easiest butterfly to identify and to find. It is also easy to collect the eggs and raise them through the complete metamorphosis. The monarch butterfly is somewhere between 3¹/₂ to 4 inches long. It is an orange and black butterfly: the wings are predominately orange with heavy black rims around the entire front and back wing. There are black veins through the orange and some white spots in the outside black edge. On the hind wing of the male, on one of the main midribs, there is a dark spot—this is a scent gland used in mating to attract a female. The female lacks this spot. The monarch is apparently not a tasty morsel for birds because they leave it alone.

The monarch is one of the most common butterflies because the larvae feed mainly on milkweed or any of the milkweed family. Sometimes monarchs are even called milkweed butterflies. The eggs on the milkweed leaves look like tiny white dots. If you look at them with a magnifier, they look like white hand grenades. The eggs hatch in a few days and small worms with alternating stripes of orange, black, and white appear and start to eat the leaf of the milkweed. They have two antennae in front and two behind. The worm will keep growing and living on the same plant. (Milkweed plants may have as

**Monarch,
continued**

many as fifteen to twenty caterpillars on them.) When it gets big enough it crawls to a leaf or another part of the plant where it attaches itself, sheds its outer skin, and turns itself into a light green chrysalis with gold spots about one inch long. This is the pupa or resting stage. In seven to fifteen days the chrysalis turns into the butterfly.

The monarch butterfly is one of the butterflies that migrates, leaving parts of North America and flying south. Only in recent years have we found that it really migrates and where it migrates to. The monarch flies to parts of Mexico, California, Florida and some of the Gulf states where it overwinters. As spring approaches it comes back, laying eggs along the way that produce broods of monarch caterpillars.

Viceroy
page 117

The viceroy butterfly is basically a mimic of the monarch. Although it can easily be distinguished from the monarch by its markings and size it does have the same basic orange, black, and white colors, which probably help it fool predators that don't like the taste of the monarch. The viceroy can be distinguished by the black lines across the back wings parallel to the outer edge of the wings. It is also smaller, ranging from 2$\frac{1}{2}$ to 3 inches wide. The viceroy is partial to feeding on willow and poplar leaves.

Buckeye
page 117

Buckeye butterflies are brightly colored with different shades of orange and brown. They measure from 2 to 2$\frac{1}{4}$ inches. The outer portions of both the hind wing and fore wing have large "eyes" as part of the coloration. These black eye spots with a blue center give the impression of a larger animal or bird looking back at a possible predator, dissuading it from eating the buckeye. The eye spots are often surrounded with black and then a light color to accent them, especially on the fore wing.

The buckeyes are one of the few butterflies that overwinter as adults. They stay under leaf litter in the cold season; in warm months they can be found in most weed fields or in yards that haven't been mown recently. They also can be found visiting many of the flowers we have in our gardens.

Crescent
page 118

The crescents are orange or yellow-brown over all with dramatic black streaks parallel to the edge of the wings. They range from 1 to 1³/₄ inches in width. They are called crescents because of the pale yellow C-shaped mark on the undersides of the hind wings. Occasionally these crescent marks are multiple. Some crescent butterflies have wider bands of black throughout the orange. If these bands are very large, orange spots can appear inside the black. The underside of the wings is much more brightly colored than the upper side. When resting, the butterfly keeps its wings folded over its back. Crescents are attracted to most any flower found in our yards.

Mourning Cloak
page 118

The mourning cloak, from 3 to 3¹/₂ inches wide, is one of the tortoise shells, a group of butterflies with tortoise-shell scallopings along the edges of the wings. The mourning cloak is easily recognized by the bright yellow rim on both the fore wing and rear wing, lined on the inside with a broad black band with blue spots in it. The remainder of the wing is a very rich brown with some yellow spots in the fore wing.

The adult mourning cloak is our earliest spring butterfly; it overwinters in forests under leaves, debris, and logs, coming out very early in the spring on nice sunny days. The host plants for this butterfly are elm, willow, and poplar, so it is often found in or near wet forests.

Red Admiral
page 117

The admirals are easily recognized butterflies because of the bright band of color going through an otherwise dark wing. The red admiral is no exception. The outer portion of the upper wings is black with some white spots. A bright orange or reddish band goes through the wings from the front of the fore wing all the way to the back of the hind wing. On the hind wing, the reddish orange band becomes the outer edge of the wing and the insides of the wing are entirely black. The red admiral's width is from 1 1/2 to 2 1/2 inches.

The best known host plants for the red admiral are different types of nettles. Occasionally red admirals will overwinter as adults, but most often they overwinter as chrysalises. Some red admirals migrate as well. They are very tame butterflies, often alighting on your nice warm shirt as you work in the garden.

Common Blue or Spring Azure
page 117

The blues are very small butterflies, rarely getting to be more than one inch and often less than one-half inch. As their name indicates they are blue butterflies. The blue color is usually only found on the upper side of the wings, while the undersides have a pretty speckling of light browns and grays with rows of dots along the outer edges of the wings.

We often see the common blue or spring azure in early spring. It is almost entirely blue. The females of the common blue are generally a darker blue than the males to begin with, but as summer progresses the females become lighter and both sexes look the same. Some of the common blues may have brightly colored borders on the edge of their wings along with spots in various colors such as browns, oranges, and yellows. This is probably one of our prettiest butterflies although it is very small. The spring azure secretes a liquid called honeydew that attracts ants. It feeds on the nectar of most any flowering plant.

Coppers
page 117

The coppers are brightly colored butterflies, usually very small—from 1 to $1^3/_4$ inches. They are a coppery orange color over most of the wings with variations of lines and spots of black. The undersides of most coppers are a pale tan to buff spotted with brown and often outlined in white or yellow. The underside is often as striking as the upper wing.

The American copper is the most common variety. The food plant for the larva is sheep sorrel, and the adults can be attracted to the flowers in our yards, especially the yellow ones.

Whites
page 115

The whites are easily recognized butterflies: one-quarter to two inches in width, they are predominately white, though the fore wings often have black spots and lines bordering the edges. The spots can be large or small, and sometimes spots are lacking altogether. Only occasionally are the hind wings spotted. Sometimes the underside of the whites can be a creamy to a yellow color, but most often they are white on both sides. Female whites will usually have more black markings than the males.

The whites include many of the butterflies that damage our vegetable crops, such as the cabbage butterfly. Its larva is a green caterpillar that attacks cabbages and related plants. Because of its coloring it is not easily noticed and causes extensive damage to the outer leaves. It can be controlled by removing the caterpillar or by using insecticides.

Sulphurs
page 117

The sulphurs are a little larger than the whites, ranging from $1^1/_4$ to $3^1/_4$ inches. They are bright sulphur yellow, usually on both the underside and the upper part of the wings. They can have black markings bordering the edge of the wings and black spots on the fore wings. Often the yellow will grade into orange toward the edge. Any spots on the orange will be dark brown instead of black.

The sulphurs are usually not as much of a threat to our vegetable crops as the whites, but they can cause some problems to our grass and pea crops. The sleepy sulphur is common and can be seen in good numbers around standing water such as birdbaths.

• • • • • • • SWALLOWTAILS • • • • • • •

Swallowtails are the largest group of butterflies commonly seen in the eastern United States. They range in size from $2^1/2$ inches to over 6 inches. Swallowtails are shaped much as their name indicates, with a long teardrop-shaped projection off the hind wing that resembles the tail of a swallow. Sometimes they have more than one projection. The wings, especially the hind wings, are scalloped. Black is the most prevalent color, striped and spotted with bright yellows, blues, oranges, and reds, though yellow is most common. The females and males may have different colorations and may differ in size.

The swallowtail larvae or caterpillars feed mainly on shrubs and trees. They are smooth-bodied caterpillars, and though the different species are colored differently, most of them have two horn-like projections behind the head. When these caterpillars are picked up an odor can be detected. This odor has even caused some people to vomit. Swallowtail caterpillars most often make a chrysalis and overwinter in the chrysalis stage. Very rarely does the swallowtail overwinter as an adult.

Pipevine Swallowtail
page 118

The pipevine swallowtail feeds on the pipevine in southeastern North America. It is a fairly large butterfly, up to $4^1/2$ inches long. Very dark for a swallowtail, it has fore wings of a heavy, rich brown bordered in white, blue, and green spots. The hind wings, the ones with the swallowtail projections, are usually a deep blue bordered in white and brown. The pipevine swallowtail's eggs are easy to find on pipevines and snakeroot because they are bright orange and are laid in clusters.

Yellow or Tiger Swallowtail
page 118

The tiger swallowtails are the largest yellow swallowtails. They are predominately yellow whereas most other swallowtails are predominately black. They are called tiger swallowtails because of the tigerlike black stripes crossing the wings. The fore

Yellow or Tiger
Swallowtail,
continued

wings are bordered in spots of yellow, black, and brown and the hind wings have borders in deep rich orange and blue. The eastern tiger swallowtail can be up to six inches in length. Sometimes you will find a female tiger swallowtail that is almost all brown. The tail markings on the hind wing are very similar in both the yellow and brown phases.

The yellow swallowtail feeds on willow and poplar and makes one-leaf nests in these trees. This is where the larvae begin foraging. Two to three life cycles occur each summer, the butterflies overwinter as pupae, and adults emerge in early spring.

Black Swallowtail
page 118

The black swallowtail is a more typical swallowtail. It is predominately black with rows of yellow dots and spots going from the fore wing to the inner part of the hind wing. The hind wing may also have spots and blotches of orange and blue. The black swallowtail is a little smaller than the tiger swallowtail, about $2^1/2$ to $3^1/2$ inches.

Black swallowtails can be found feeding on nectar on most any of the plants in our garden. They like sunny open areas. The eggs are easily identified: they are bright yellow and are usually laid on Queen Anne's Lace, celery, parsnips, and carrots.

Skippers
page 118

Skippers are small butterflies. Their name comes from their habitual flight that skips from one place to the next. Most of the skippers are a dull brown to gray and range from one-half to two inches wide. They have lines of dots and blotches along the outer edges of the wings. The dots can be black, dark brown, buff, tan, and even white. Occasionally you will find skippers with white on the trailing edge of the wings. The skippers are easily distinguished from other butterflies by their thin antennae, which end in a little club that is curved downward. The larvae like to feed on grasses and weeds in fields, so they are not serious pests to our gardens and yards.

The long-tailed skipper, also called the bean leaf roller, has large white spots on the fore wing and a long tail. The larvae feed on bean plants. It is one of the fastest-flying skippers and is fairly common in the southeastern part of North America.

• • • • • MOTHS AND CATERPILLARS • • • • •

Moths are a little different from butterflies; they have larger and fatter bodies and different antennae. The antennae of moths usually have filaments at the end. The antennae can vary dramatically in shape, some being very ornate, but they lack the club shape at the end that some butterflies have. When resting, moths normally hold their wings flat or fold them close to the body. They do not hold them erect over the top of their body in the manner of most butterflies.

Many moth larvae spin a cocoon rather than constructing a chrysalis. They secrete a strand of silk from their lower lip and weave it around themselves. The caterpillar may emerge from this cocoon in anywhere from a week to six months depending on the species. We can see moths most often in the evening feeding on flowers. Many are also attracted to our lights during the night. Moth larvae are often given credit for damaging fruit and vegetable crops, but they probably do not cause any more damage than do butterfly larvae.

Luna Moth
page 119

The luna is one of the prettiest moths that we find flying around our porch light or yard light at night. The luna moth is a greenish blue with long trailing tails and two spots on the hind wings resembling eyes. It ranges from three to almost five inches wide. The antennae are canoe-shaped and very heavily fila-mented. The luna moth has been called the white bat because it appears during the evening hours flying lazily along the edges of yards and fields.

The larvae feed mainly on trees, especially sweet gum, hickory, and birch. Their large papery cocoon is usually spun on the ground with a few leaves wrapped around it.

Polyphemus Moth
page 119

The polyphemus moth is another one of our large moths, reaching $3^1/2$ to almost 6 inches in length. The polyphemus moth is very striking: it is a rich

**Polyphemus Moth,
continued**

light brown, and bordering the hind wing and fore wing are stripes of deep brown, tan, or white. The antennae of the polyphemus are canoe-shaped like those of the luna. Filaments begin very narrow at the tip, get wider, then narrow again at the head. The fore wings often have a tiny white eye spot in the center. The hind wing has a huge eye spot with a yellow marking inside somewhat reminiscent of a large beetle with a yellow head. This single eye spot gives the moth its name; Polyphemus was the one-eyed cyclops met by Odysseus.

The larvae of the polyphemus like to feed on trees and shrubs. In the north part of the country they like the box elder tree and elderberry shrub; in other parts of the country they feed on trees such as hickory, elm, maple, and birch. The polyphemus moth is one of the silkworm moths—the larvae produce silken cocoons.

Tiger Moth (Woolly Bear Caterpillar)
page 119

Tiger moths are small to medium-size moths ranging from just under one inch to over three inches in width. Several characteristics distinguish them from other types of moths. These characteristics are important because of the great variability in coloration that tiger moths may have. Both fore wing and hind wing are quite narrow. The width of the moth with its wings outspread is generally less than the length of the body. The antennae of the tiger moth are very thinly filamented. Another distinguishing characteristic is the square looking abdomen. The abdomen is not actually squared off, but tiny hairs at the end make it appear to be.

The common tiger moths are striped with yellow and black or orange and black and have orange underwings. The striping is quite varied, crisscrossing back and forth with no evident pattern. The hind wing often has no striping, just black and orange spotting; the black spots are outlined with yellow. Although there are many other variations, all tiger moths have the same basic wing shapes with some

Tiger Moth,
continued

type of black and yellow markings. The underwings are a different color than the upper wings.

One moth not easily recognized as a tiger moth is the fall webworm. Webworms spin a nest of webbing over a branch of leaves and the larvae inside eat the leaves. They do both their spinning and feeding during the daytime, as opposed to a tent caterpillar which comes out to feed only at night. The fall webworm moth is a small white moth. Its body and wings are entirely white. Occasionally they may have spots on the fore wings.

The tiger moth caterpillars are commonly covered with hair and curl up when disturbed. The woolly bear caterpillar is the most common example. Many of the tiger moth larvae, including the woolly bear, overwinter as caterpillars, although some spin a cocoon using their body hairs to line the cocoon.

The woolly bear or banded woolly bear is a very hairy caterpillar commonly found around our yard, especially in the fall. It is easy to recognize: black on both ends with a brown band in its midsection. It overwinters as an adult caterpillar and spins a cocoon in the last part of the winter or early spring, using all the hair from its outer body. The tiger moth that emerges from the woolly bear's cocoon is called the Isabella moth. It is one of the smaller tiger moths and is yellowish with spots on the body and wings. It has been said that the woolly bear can predict the severity of winter, depending upon how much black or brown is found in its hair. (Supposedly a wide brown band means a mild winter, but if black dominates the winter will be harsh. But don't put too much faith in this legend.)

Hawk Moth or Sphinx Moth
page 119
(Tomato Horn Worm
page 115)

The hawk moth is probably one of the fattest bodied moths we see. It has a protective coloration of black and brown, resembling dead leaves. Hawk moths range from three to five inches in size. The underwings, the second pair of wings, and the abdomen may sport colors ranging from blue to violet to pink to orange. The name hawk moth comes from their narrow, pointed wings which often give a hawklike impression. The sphinx appellation comes from the larva's habit of holding its head up and away from its body like the great statue of the Sphinx. Sometimes these moths are called hummingbird moths because of their very rapid and direct flight. They take nectar from flowers using their long, coiled proboscis.

The larvae are fat bodied, usually smooth skinned, and generally green. The tomato horn worm is probably the most common of these and is considered a pest in gardens. It is a smooth green worm two to four inches in length and is very segmented. The easiest way to recognize the worm is by the long horn located at the rear that is usually reddish in color with a red border. It also has black and white stripes with little eye spots along the sides of the green body.

This worm can be a serious pest on tomatoes. The adult moth lays its eggs on the leaves; when the tomato horn worm hatches it eats the new and tender leaves of the tomato and sometimes pepper plants. One caterpillar will eat a good portion of a tomato plant in just a week. The easiest method of control is to detect the foraging, find the worm, and remove it from the plant. Simply look for newly chewed plants or for the worms' biscuitlike droppings, especially the fresher, greener droppings on the ground beneath the plant. Because the worm is green, it is sometimes very difficult to locate.

Occasionally you will find the horn worm with white egg capsules on it. These are from the braconid wasp, a tomato horn worm parasite. Do not destroy these caterpillars because allowing the wasp to reproduce helps control the worms. The horn worm will eventually die as the braconid larvae hatch and feed upon it.

Underwing Moth
page 119

The underwings are 2 to 3 1/2 inches long. They are similar to the hawk moth in that the fore wings have a protective pattern of varied browns, blacks, and tans that resembles tree bark or dead leaves. The wings of the underwing moth are much larger than those of the hawk moth. The hind wings have spectacular coloration when the moth is in flight: bands of black and brown with alternating bands of bright colors such as orange, yellow, white, and silver.

The underwing larvae usually also have excellent protective coloration matching dead branches or leaves. They feed mainly on trees and shrubs. The underwings are summertime moths; they overwinter as eggs and the larvae hatch in the springtime. The larvae feed, pupate, then turn into the underwing moths during the summer. They are fun to watch because they are so well camouflaged. When they fly through the air, the colorful underwings are very noticeable, but as soon as it lands on the bark of a tree, it becomes instantaneously hidden and almost impossible to find. Underwings are not a serious pest to trees and shrubs.

Tent Caterpillar
page 113

The tent caterpillar is a very small moth, generally a deep rich brown in color, with light stripes across the fore wings. The fat body tapers at the abdomen to a square end.

The tent caterpillar's moth lays its eggs on a branch of a host tree in a foamy, shiny mass. The eggs remain there over the winter, and in early spring the caterpillars hatch. The tent caterpillar is easily recognized during the spring when it weaves its nests made of silken threads in the crotches of trees. Fifty to three hundred tent caterpillars hide in the tent during the daytime; at night they leave its protection and crawl up the branches to the ends to feed on the leaves. Wild black cherry and other fruit trees are common host trees. In early to midsummer they build their cocoons.

**Tent Caterpillar,
continued**

Tent caterpillars are hairy and therefore unappetizing to most birds; the only two species known to eat them are the yellow-billed and black-billed cuckoos. Therefore the caterpillars are not easily controlled. The tent generally has to be destroyed by cutting the branch away or burning the nest because the caterpillars hide inside, and even sprays are difficult to get through the silk material. In small trees this insect can be a serious pest, causing complete defoliation. Unless this occurs persistently over two or three springs, however, the tent caterpillar will not fatally harm the tree.

Rosy Maple Moth
page 119

The rosy maple is one of the most common moths found on sugar maple trees. Its habitat extends throughout the eastern United States. This moth is from one to two inches long. It is mostly yellow with some orange and purple markings on the fore wings. The moths can live in large colonies and in some areas have been known to completely denude a maple tree in summertime, but they are usually harmless.

The caterpillar is predominantly green with light striping along the sides. Because it feeds on maple leaves, especially the sugar maple, it is called the green striped maple worm. Rather than spinning a cocoon, the caterpillars burrow into the ground to pupate. They can easily be raised indoors if enough soil is provided for them.

Royal Walnut Moth
page 119

This moth is fairly large, from $3^1/2$ to $5^1/2$ inches long. The royal walnut moth is yellow overall with reddish brown scales covering the parallel veins in the wings. These veins run from the joint of the wings to the tip. Bright yellow spots are scattered throughout the duskier brown color.

The royal walnut moth resides anywhere you find hickory trees because the caterpillar feeds on its leaves. The caterpillar is called the hickory horned devil because it has a number of projections on the front part of its body that are curved like horns. These horns are bright orange with black tips and make it look extremely ferocious. The caterpillar is fat bodied and very hairy.

Clothes Moths
page 112

This group contains many moths that eat household items made from wool, silk, and cotton. They also can be a pest in furs and other organic materials, including feathers. These moths are generally small, from one-quarter inch to just over one-half inch long.

The adult moth is a light brown. The only one that is easily recognized from the other moths is the carpet moth, which has blackish brown on the fore wing close to the body.

Moths have complete metamorphoses. It is the larval stage that causes the most damage: the worm or caterpillar feasts on carpeting or clothing. The moth larva often makes its presence known by spinning small silk webs on clothing where it can eat and be protected. The caterpillar can be small, from $1/16$ to $1/2$ inch long. Its presence usually is not noticed until holes are found in our belongings.

Placing mothballs in all containers where clothes are stored is a good method of protection. Regular cleaning and washing of fabrics will also keep the moth buildup from occurring. The young larvae laid by the adult moth mature for a few days to a week before beginning to eat the fabric, so normal washings should be sufficient to keep the moth population under control.

CHAPTER SIX

TREES AND SHRUBS

Just what is a tree and what is a shrub? Normally we define trees as woody plants with a stout main stem or trunk at least three inches in diameter. A shrub usually has multiple stems originating from a single root source and generally stays under twelve to thirty feet in height.

There are over seven hundred native North American trees, plus many non-native trees brought into the United States. Trees are most easily identified by overall shape, bark pattern, and leaf shape. Fruit and flowers also help identify a tree when they are present.

Trees are divided into two basic groups: evergreen and deciduous. Those that keep their leaves all year are the evergreens like pines, spruces, firs, arborvitaes, cedars, and junipers. Those that lose their leaves in winter, or whose leaves turn brown, are deciduous. (There are some trees that, although they are related to evergreens, lose their needles during the wintertime.)

In this chapter, each category will be broken down according to the arrangement of the leaves or needles: whether the leaves or needles are in groups, single, or scattered. In deciduous trees the leaves can be broken down even further. They can be compound or simple, with smooth edges or uneven edges. When identifying trees, use the process of elimination. First determine whether it is a deciduous tree or an evergreen. Then take a look at the leaves or needles.

EVERGREENS

The evergreen trees, which include pines, hemlocks, spruces, and firs, produce cones. These cones have seeds in them that are covered by hard scales arising from a central stalk. The scales overlap to protect the seeds and keep them from being dried out during the harsh winters. The seeds underneath these scales generally have a fruiting portion located at the end of a wing. This wing allows the seed to spin or float down to the ground some distance away from the parent tree.

The characteristic shape of cones is generally elliptical with a pointed end. Different types of evergreens have different cone shapes, from long and narrow to short and fat, so the cone is one way of identifying the tree. The position of the cone on the branch can also distinguish the species.

Some cones require specific conditions to open, such as a period of cold or dry weather, or in some cases, like the jack pine, a very hot temperature such as a forest fire. The cones open up after the heat of the fire and drop the seeds, allowing the new seedlings to grow.

Pines
page 120

Pine trees belong to the conifer family, which means they produce cones instead of flowers. The needles appear in clusters; pine trees have needles of varying lengths in groups of two to five.

A characteristic of pine trees is the terminal bud at the end of each twig that produces the new stem. Lateral buds are located beside the terminal bud and they produce stems that grow perpendicular to the terminal bud and the main stem. When the tree limb stops growing at the end of the summer, a new cluster of buds will grow. You can therefore infer what the growing year was like by the distance between the whorls of branches, thus you can determine quite accurately the age of the pine tree. Pine trees have soft wood and are often grown for lumber because of their rapid growth rate.

Spruces
page 120

Spruce trees, another member of the conifer group, usually have straight vertical trunks. Their lower branches are more tolerant of shade than other evergreens and remain growing throughout the life of the tree, in contrast with other trees whose lower branches die due to lack of sunlight. Spruce tree needles grow singly, usually on a little woody pedestal that remains after the needles fall. The needle of a spruce is four-sided, in the shape of a parallelogram, and quite stiff and sharp. The needles grow around the whole stem instead of lying along any particular plane on the stem as in firs. The cones hang downward from the branches.

Spruces are more common in the northern United States, although they can be transplanted to the

Spruces,
continued

south. Two of the spruces common in our yards are the blue spruce, an ornamental tree with a characteristic bluish gray hue, and the Norway spruce, a European tree with branches that hang downward and that retain their needles all the way to the ground. Two other species found predominantly in the north are the white spruce and the black spruce. The white spruce is an upland variety whereas the black spruce grows mainly in bogs. In the eastern United States, spruces rarely get above sixty to eighty feet. Many animals make use of the needles and the seeds in the cones. Squirrels and some birds use the seeds as a food source.

Firs
page 120

Fir trees have flat, relatively soft needles; this has given them the nickname "flat friendly fir." The tip of the needle is generally square and the underside is often a silvery color. The needles usually grow on the sides of the branch instead of encircling it. When a fir needle is broken off it leaves the branch smooth or with a slight depression, just the opposite of the woody stalk left on a spruce. Fir trees do not grow branches as thickly as spruce. The cones grow upwards from the branch.

Two common kinds of fir are the balsam fir and the Douglas fir. The balsam fir is a smaller tree, growing to sixty feet at the most. The Douglas fir, especially on the west coast, gets to be a fairly large tree, exceeding one hundred feet. The bark of balsam and Douglas firs has little blisters or bumps that can pop open to release a resin, sometimes rather abruptly. These blisters are characteristic of the fir tree. Years ago the resin was used in microscope lenses and for mounting microscopic slides because it is optically clear.

Cedars
page 120

Cedars have evergreenlike needles that actually are flat scales laid one on top of the other. Some people grow white cedars as a hedge because their needles

Cedars, continued

are so thick. The most common cedar found in the United States is the white cedar, though it is more widespread in the north. The white cedar grows best in wet areas. It is used for food by many animals, especially deer which forage on it extensively during the winter. White cedars can grow to be quite large, reaching heights of seventy-five to eighty-five feet. The cones of the white cedar are round, sometimes glossy, and blue or purple in color.

Juniper or Red Cedar
page 120

Junipers are found throughout the eastern United States but are more common in the southern range. They can adapt themselves to soils that are very rocky and not terribly rich. Instead of cones they produce berries, which are generally blue or black in color and have the characteristics of tiny cones. Junipers are similar to cedars in that they have a scalelike foliage; generally the last scale is pointed and sharp. Junipers are small, often looking more like bushes than trees. The berries are a good food source for birds in the winter. Birds that eat juniper berries include cedar waxwings, bluebirds, robins, and mockingbirds.

Hemlock
page 120

In the eastern part of the United States, the eastern hemlock is found mainly in the states bordering the Great Lakes and those with mountainous regions such as in the Appalachians and parts of Pennsylvania. Hemlocks like a cool environment and therefore usually grow on north-facing slopes. They also prefer moist soil. Hemlocks can grow between fifty and seventy-five feet tall. They have short needles, usually less than one-quarter inch. The needles are flat and of varying lengths on the stem. The underside of the needles has a whitish green cast and the upper surface is dark green. When the wind blows, the whitish green undersides are quite noticeable. The cones are small, usually under one-half inch in length, and are found at the tips of the branches.

The branches of a hemlock are quite limber. The topmost branch does not point straight up like most of the pines; it is usually bent over. The hemlock is often grown in yards because the lower branches will stay green even in the shade of the upper branches.

DECIDUOUS TREES

Broadleaved trees are deciduous trees; they lose their leaves in the winter. These trees will be discussed according to leaf type since this is the major characteristic used in identifying tree species. The first section deals with trees that have compound leaves. This means there is more than one leaflet on the leaf stalk. Leaflets are distinguished from leaves by the absence of a bud. Leaves have buds; compound leaves with leaflets have buds, but the individual leaflets on a compound leaf do not.

The opposite of a compound leaf is a simple leaf: a leaf with a single blade for each stalk. Simple leaves may be smooth-edged or they may have teeth or lobes (large, irregular projections) on the edges.

• • • • • • COMPOUND LEAVES • • • • • •

Black Walnut
page 121

The black walnut's compound leaves alternate on the branch instead of being opposite each other. The leaflets, however, are opposite each other on the leaf stem and occasionally a small leaflet is located at the very tip of the leaf. The leaves are one to two feet long. The black walnut produces a round green fruit with a husk on the outside. The inside is comprised of a hard black shell in which the nut meat is preserved. The nut meat, eaten by humans as well as squirrels and chipmunks, has a more bitter taste than a regular walnut.

Plants will not grow near the root line of the black walnut, because it emits a substance that inhibits their growth. Avoid placing your vegetable garden close to one. Its leaves are fairly sparse, especially when it grows in the open, and it is very susceptible to fall webworm in the autumn. The falling fruit can dent cars and also make a dramatic brownish black stain in driveways.

Butternut

The butternut, or white walnut, is a very close relative of the black walnut. The easiest way to tell the two apart is by the shape of the nut. The fruit of the butternut is oblong and more egg-shaped. It is eaten by both humans and squirrels. Its leaf is similar to the black walnut's but has a large leaflet at the end.

Honey Locust
page 121

The honey locust is easily identified by the spines on the trunk and branches. Some ornamentals, however, are spineless, so another characteristic to look for is its double compound leaves. In a double compound the leaflets branch off and have leaflets of their own. The flowers of the honey locust resemble the flowers of the pea family. The fruit is a dark hanging pod growing up to one foot long and is quite prominent in the fall when the leaves are gone. The tree does not grow very tall—around fifty to eighty feet—but it grows quickly. Both the honey locust and the black locust make excellent fence posts because the wood is hard and resistant to rotting.

Black Locust
page 121

The black locust grows rapidly and is therefore often planted in yards. It has alternate compound leaves. The edges of the leaves are smooth, and each leaf has from seven to thirteen leaflets. The fruit is similar to the honey locust pods but not quite as long. The pea-shaped white flowers also resemble those of the honey locust. The black locust has spines, although not many appear on the trunk. The thorns on this tree are at the base of the leaves and are very regular and short.

The black locust is one of the favorite trees of an insect called the walking stick. They can sometimes number in the hundreds on one tree. The black locust is smaller than the honey locust; it grows thirty to fifty feet high. It is commonly found only in the middle states but is being planted in other areas and has escaped to fence rows and ditches throughout the eastern United States.

Horse Chestnut

The horse chestnut is no longer a common native of the eastern United States because of the horse chestnut blight that eradicated the trees in the early part of the twentieth century. But many horse chestnuts are being replanted and are making a comeback. The horse chestnuts still in existence range from fifty to seventy-five feet tall.

The horse chestnut has leaves that are compound and opposite. The compound leaflets are whorled, meaning they have anywhere from seven to nine leaflets originating from the same spot on the petiole, the portion that attaches the leaf to the twig. The leaflets are pointed on the end and have teeth on the edges. The individual leaflets get larger towards the end. The nuts are easily recognized because they have spines all over the outer husk. These nuts are enjoyed by squirrels and other forest animals. The white flowers of the horse chestnut are erect or on spikes and have a number of flowers on one stalk.

Hickory

Hickories are large trees whose leaves are compound and alternate. Generally the leaves have five or more leaflets; the terminal leaflet is quite large. The compound leaves can range from eight to over twelve inches in length. The fruit of the hickory has a smooth outer husk. When the nut is ripe this husk breaks off freely, leaving the inner nut with its hard shell available for squirrels (especially gray squirrels) and other nut-eating animals such as deer and turkeys. The hard shell normally has a point on it and the inside fruit is quite delectable.

Hickory trees grow fifty to eighty feet tall. The wood of the hickory is light in color and hard. Pioneers used hickory wood to make handles for axes, sledge hammers, shovels, rakes, and forks. Hickories are a welcome addition to any backyard situation because they attract a good deal of wildlife.

Pecan
page 121

The pecan is predominantly a southern tree that grows fairly tall, sometimes reaching 125 to 140 feet. The leaves are compound and alternate with eight to fifteen fine-toothed leaflets. The leaflets grow progressively larger away from the petiole. Pecan trees produce the familiar pecan nut. The nut has a thin husk over it and as the fruit matures the husk breaks off in four pieces, leaving the inner smooth, brown shell of the pecan. With a little care, pecans can be grown in northern backyards, not only providing us with nuts but also attracting squirrels and other wildlife. Pecans like rich soil that is not too wet. The wood, although not as hard as walnut, is just as pretty.

Box Elder
page 121

The box elder, also called the ash leaf maple, actually belongs to the maple family although it has opposite compound leaves. The leaves have anywhere from three to seven small leaflets with fairly large teeth. The new stems have a whitish cast. The seeds look very similar to maple seeds: winged with a fat pod at the end. Box elders only reach about twenty-five to fifty feet in height.

Despite its leaf pattern the box elder is a true maple and can be tapped for sap to make maple syrup. The box elder tree grows along ditches and wet areas along the edges of our yards. It is not a popular tree to plant for ornamental use, although it grows rapidly, because of its tendency to send up a number of branches or shoots, which make it look more like a shrub than a tree. By careful pruning you can make the box elder into a decent shade tree for your backyard.

Mountain Ash
page 121

The mountain ash is actually not an ash: it is in the rose family and is related to the apple and hawthorn. It has an alternate compound leaf with thirteen to seventeen leaflets exhibiting small teeth. The compound leaves are large, often over one foot in length. The mountain ash has white flowers in clusters at the top of the tree and reddish orange berries in the fall that are heavy and bend downward. Birds, squirrels, and other animals feast on the berries during the winter. In the wild, moose and deer eat both the branches and the berries.

The mountain ash is a small tree, usually not growing above thirty feet and producing little shade. Many people even consider it a shrub. The mountain ash is found in the northern part of the eastern United States growing wild as well as cultivated in backyards. One ornamental type of mountain ash comes from Europe and has a more orangish berry than the native mountain ash.

White Ash
page 121

The white ash is one of our common ash trees and is often found in our yards. It grows fairly tall, sometimes as high as one hundred feet. The bark is deeply grooved and resembles a tire tread. White ashes have opposite compound leaves, normally with seven leaflets that are uniform in size. The leaflets have shallow irregular teeth on them. The seeds are single-winged, similar to maple seeds, except they are very straight and pointed rather like a bullet. The seed portion is on one end of the wing. They spin to the ground in the fall. Although ash trees are not great shade trees they attract many birds, particularly pine siskins and grosbeaks, which eat the seeds during the winter. Chipmunks and squirrels also use the seeds for their wintertime food. White ash trees are valued highly for the strength of the wood, which is commonly used for baseball bats and tool handles.

• • • SIMPLE LEAVES WITH SMOOTH EDGES • • •

Magnolia
page 122

Magnolias have large leaves anywhere from five to eight inches long. The leaves are oval and have very smooth edges. Its large pink or white flowers bloom early in the spring. Magnolias can become quite large, as high as seventy-five feet if they are grown in the wild. In our yards they normally remain under twenty-five to thirty-five feet. The buds of the magnolia are easily recognized. They are shaped like tiny, somewhat flattened footballs and are one-half to two inches long with a fuzzy surface.

The magnolia is predominately a southern tree, although a number have been planted as ornamentals in the northern part of the country. Many of the magnolias we see in the north are cultivated magnolias, a cross between a native magnolia and one from China or the Far East. Pink blossoms are usually a product of cultivated magnolias.

Flowering Dogwood
page 122

The flowering dogwood can be found over most of the eastern United States. The dogwood tree has a smooth-edged leaf that is opposite, which means the leaflets grow directly across from each other on the stem. In spring it develops white leaves that look like flower petals because they are notched at the end rather than pointed. In the middle of these white leaves the actual blossom is found. The flower is usually yellow, or sometimes pink, and rather inconspicuous. The dogwood also produces clusters of red berries in the fall that are relished by birds and small animals.

This small tree, which grows to twenty-five feet at the most, is normally found in the understory of the forest. It adapts well to our yards, especially if it is placed underneath the shade of another tree, such as a maple. The branches of the flowering dogwood are arranged in layers, an adaptation to living beneath other trees. It produces a canopy or umbrella of leaves so that it can catch as much sunlight as possible as it filters down through the trees.

Live Oak
page 122

The live oak is a common tree in the southeastern United States. The oblong leaves are relatively small, usually from two to five inches, and stay green for most of the winter, giving the appearance that the tree is alive and growing. The upper part of the leaf is dark green and the underside looks silvery green because of the hair underneath. The acorn is very dark, sometimes almost black.

The live oak is a good shade tree because the branches begin to spread out a short distance up the trunk. It often seems wider than it is tall since it does not reach great heights, usually between thirty and forty-five feet. Live oaks can live in dry areas better than most other deciduous trees. They adapt well and are found quite often on southern sandy coasts. They are popular with wildlife, which eat the acorns and use the cover of the tree for protection and nesting. Like other oaks they bear yellow male catkins and tiny green female flowers on the same tree.

• • • • **SIMPLE LEAVES WITH LOBES** • • • •

Oaks
page 122

Oak trees can be found over the entire eastern United States. They grow relatively slowly but are long-lived and eventually reach heights of 80 to 120 feet and develop very thick trunks. Oak leaves alternate on the branch and have five to seven deep lobes. Many oaks do not lose all their leaves in the winter. They usually, with the exception of the pin oak, are not as colorful as the maples during the fall, turning predominantly brown and yellow.

The most common oaks in the eastern region are the white oak, red oak, black oak, and pin oak. The white oak is fairly easy to identify because of its bark, which is scaled and light gray. The leaves of the white oak have rounded or smooth ends on the lobes.

The lobes of the red oak leaf have points or spines on them. Red oak bark has fissures with wide spaces between, somewhat resembling ski trails.

Black oak leaves also have spines on the lobes, but the lobes are more irregular, more deeply cut, narrow, and unevenly spaced. The bark of a black oak is generally dark, almost black, with alternating fissures and raised portions.

Pin oaks have smaller leaves that are deeply pointed with very narrow lobes. The pin oak can become quite brightly colored in autumn. Pin oaks are most easily identified by their branches, which bend or point downward from the trunk.

The white oak's acorn tastes fairly good to people as well as wild animals, but the nuts of the red, black, and pin oaks are bitter. Squirrels and other animals like turkeys and deer will eat the less tasty acorns in the last part of winter. Large oak trees, especially those that have outreaching branches, often provide homes for raccoons or opossums during the summer, as well as numerous birds and squirrels.

Mulberry
page 123

The mulberry has a heart-shaped leaf generally ranging from three to five inches with short, blunt teeth. Usually the leaves are lobed. The lobes can be deep or almost nonexistent depending on the individual tree. Mulberries have orangish bark that is relatively smooth.

There are three varieties of mulberry in the eastern United States. They are named according to the color of the fruit: red mulberry, white mulberry, and black mulberry. The oblong black mulberry is actually a deep purple. Mulberry fruits attract lots of birds in the summertime. They are quite edible and are delicious in pies and jams.

Mulberries are sometimes planted inadvertently in our yard by birds that drop the seeds. They do not get very large, between thirty and fifty feet tall. In some parts of the world, though not the United States, mulberry leaves are used to feed silkworms. Mulberries grow quite rapidly, spreading out and making fairly wide shade trees.

Maples
page 123

Maples have leaves shaped like the palm of a person's hand, usually with five lobes. Very large teeth may be present at the end of each lobe and there may be secondary teeth along the large teeth. The leaves grow in pairs opposite each other on the stem. The maples are one of the first trees to bloom in the springtime and produce green to greenish yellow male and female flowers on separate branches.

The seeds, called samaras, are very distinctive. There are wings attached to the seed pod that are wide at the end and narrower near the base where the seed is located. They grow in pairs hanging down from the branch. As they fall off the tree in early to midsummer they spin and are often likened to helicopter blades. The seeds are eaten and collected for winter storage by many small animals such as chipmunks, white-footed mice, and red squirrels.

Maples are slow-growing trees but eventually reach heights of thirty to eighty feet. They make excellent shade trees because they become quite broad if grown in the open and have dense foliage. They also provide homes for a variety of wildlife. Maple wood is extremely hard and can be used for furniture as well as flooring. It is relatively light in color and is a fine wood to have in your home.

There are five species of maple common in eastern North America: red maple, sugar maple, silver maple, Norway maple, and black maple. The red maple leaf has a relatively wide center lobe with many secondary teeth along the sides. The sugar maple also has a wide central lobe, but it lacks secondary teeth. The central lobe on the silver maple narrows as it nears the side lobes, and the leaf has a silvery cast underneath. The Norway maple and

Maples,
continued

black maple are similar to the sugar maple: the leaf has few secondary teeth and is generally wider than it is long. It usually has only three lobes; if there are five, the bottom two lobes are quite small. The cultivated varieties have purplish or dark purple leaves.

All maples produce a sugar-rich sap that, when tapped, is made into maple syrup and sugar. The sugar maple, Norway maple, and black maple are the most commonly tapped trees. Silver maple and red maple can also be tapped, but their season is shorter because they bloom earlier. The amount of sugar produced depends on each individual tree, not necessarily on the species.

The silver maple is probably the maple most often planted in yards because unlike the other species it grows rather quickly. However, it has the shortest life span, usually about twenty to fifty years, as opposed to the other species that can endure for centuries.

Maple trees exhibit fantastic fall colors. The leaves turn all different shades of red, yellow, and orange depending on their summer growth. Healthy growth produces brilliant pigments.

Sycamore
page 123

Sycamores have maple-shaped leaves that grow alternately and are quite large, about six or seven inches across. They may be identified very easily by the seed pods, which are brown balls about the size of golf balls that hang down from the branches. The bark is also distinctive. It peels off in large patches leaving a gray or whitish bark underneath that becomes blotched in the sunlight. The top of the sycamore tree has more white bark because the brown is more easily blown away by the wind and the sun hits more evenly.

When they grow naturally sycamores usually prefer to be near waterways. But they are often planted in cities and yards because they are fairly fast-growing, provide good shade, and grow very tall, sometimes up to one hundred feet. They can also sustain themselves better in a polluted atmosphere than can most other trees.

Sweet Gum or Gum Tree
page 123

The sweet gum is found mainly in the south although it has been transplanted to the north as an ornamental tree. It derives its name from a resin that seeps from the bark when it is wounded. Indians and pioneers reportedly used this resin as chewing gum.

Gum leaves have five lobes and are similar in structure to the maple leaf. The difference is that the leaves grow alternately on the branch instead of opposite each other. The lobes have evenly spaced teeth. The star-shaped leaf can get fairly large but normally is between five and seven inches in length.

The fruiting body of the sweet gum is a spiny ball hanging down from a branch. The trees grow to about seventy-five to one hundred feet. Sweet gums usually grow in moist areas, but many have adapted to living in our yards. They produce brightly colored red, yellow, and brown leaves during the fall.

Tulip Poplar
page 123

The tulip poplar, also called yellow poplar or white wood, is found predominantly in the rich soils of the eastern United States except for the extreme northern parts of Maine, Michigan, and Wisconsin. The poplar is probably one of the easiest trees to recognize. In a forest situation it grows very tall and straight and the trunk is almost uniform in diameter from top to bottom. Mature tulip poplars measure four to six feet across and can grow over a hundred feet tall. When dried, poplar wood becomes very light in weight and is more manageable than some of the hardwoods such as oak and hickory.

The leaves are somewhat maplelike and are shaped like a cat face. They can reach from five to six inches across. The tulip poplar gets its name from the orange and green flowers growing at the ends of the branches, which look like tulips and bloom in early summer. The seed head resembles a thin pine cone with the sheaths covering the seeds. These seeds are favorites of the red squirrels. The bark is relatively thick on the new twigs. If you break a twig of tulip poplar it has a lemony smell rather like sassafras.

• • SIMPLE LEAVES WITH TOOTHED EDGES • •

Birch

Birch trees are called by a variety of names including paper birch, white birch, northern birch, and canoe birch. All these appellations refer to the same tree. Birch trees have scaled bark that is usually a striking white, sometimes with dark brown marks on it. The leaves are generally wider at the base, come to a point, and have small teeth all along the edge. Birches do not grow terribly tall, usually not more than seventy-five feet. Most often the birches in our yards grow in groups and are ornamental hybrids from Europe. These trees do not get as tall as the natives; they are usually less than fifty feet high. The other birch we may find in our yards is called the weeping birch, which has long branches that hang down. The leaves are much longer than other birch leaves.

In the spring birches produce a flower or catkin that is shaped like a tiny hot dog. It grows downward, elongates, and produces a yellow pollen. The fruit of the birch tree is a small cone rising near the place where the catkin was. Tiny winged seeds drop out of these cones later in the season; the seeds often attract siskins and other seed-eating birds. In autumn birch leaves generally turn yellow or yellow-brown.

Beech or American Beech

The beech tree has an elliptical leaf with teeth on the outer margin; each tooth has a vein leading to it. Beech trees are also recognizable by their smooth gray bark. The American beech is found over most of the eastern United States except in western areas that approach the Mississippi River valley.

**Beech or
American Beech,
continued**

In winter the beech tree produces cigar-shaped buds that are quite pointed at one end, and the bark becomes a very pronounced gray. The beech nut, which grows during the summer, has a spiny covering over it that breaks into three portions. The nut inside is triangular in shape and is readily edible by people and animals alike. In a forest the American beech gets fairly tall, well over a hundred feet with sometimes a three- to four-foot diameter. The beech is a slow-growing, long-lived tree, living up to six hundred years. In the open the beech tree provides extensive shade.

Linden or Basswood
page 124

Basswood trees get relatively tall, between seventy-five and eighty feet. The leaves are heart-shaped with pronounced teeth and are heavily veined. Lindens grow relatively quickly and produce lots of shade, and their lower branches bend or arch toward the ground. The basswood flower is quite aromatic. It grows downward on a small stem and has four, five, or six yellow to orange flowers. Each blossom grows from a leaf bract that is somewhat cigar-shaped. When the fruit, a greenish brown berry, forms and breaks off from the twig, the leaflike blade makes it spin to the ground. Linden wood is light in color and very soft, so it is perfect for carvers.

Wild Black Cherry
page 124

Black cherry tree leaves are narrow and linear with short teeth. At the base of the leaf stem are two glands or protuberances. If crushed, the leaf gives off a bad odor somewhat reminiscent of cyanide. The tree grows about seventy-five to eighty-five feet tall and has black shaggy bark. It produces a small cherry, only one-eighth to one-quarter inch across. The cherries grow in clusters and are a bluish black color when ripe.

Black cherry wood is a rich brownish red color. Wild black cherry trees can be found throughout the eastern United States and are especially common along hedgerows and fence lines. They often grow voluntarily from seeds dropped by birds and other animals.

Willow
page 124

Willows have long, narrow leaves shaped like a lance or spear head. The sides of the leaf exhibit tiny teeth and the underside is light green or gray. Often you will see appendages that look like tiny leaves at the base of the leaf; these mark it as a willow. Sometimes these appendages can be quite large and striking, surrounding the base of the leaf. Willows are generally found wherever there is water, although they have adapted to living in cultivated areas where people water them. The most common willows are the black willow and the weeping willow. The weeping willow is distinctive because the smaller branches droop down all around it. Weeping willows are ornamental trees from Asia, whereas the black willow is native.

Willows produce catkins or what we call pussy willows in the springtime. All the willows produce these catkins, though they may be different sizes and shapes. The catkins produce pollen and seeds. Willow seeds are attached to a cottony material that allows them to fly about at the end of the summer. Willows don't get terribly tall, usually around thirty to seventy feet in height before wind storms break them down. Both the bark and the wood are quite soft. The pioneers used the wood for basket making and caning. There is even a willow called the cane willow that is very pliable when wet.

Elm
page 124

Elm trees, like the willows, normally live near water but have adapted to living in our backyards. The American elm has been dramatically reduced in the eastern United States because of Dutch elm disease. The leaves are oval in shape and from three to seven inches long. The edges have double teeth that are fairly large, up to one-quarter inch long. These

**Elm,
continued**

teeth have secondary teeth on them. Another noticeable characteristic of the elm leaf is that the two halves of the leaf do not meet exactly; one half is longer than the other half. The underside of the leaf has a texture like fine sandpaper.

An elm has a tall trunk that can reach up to one hundred feet. It is V-shaped, widening at the top where the bulk of the branches are. Elms produce a round flattened seed surrounded by wings that give it a chance to fly about as it drops to the ground. Elm is a hard wood and is difficult to cut.

Cottonwood
page 124

The eastern cottonwood grows up to seventy or eighty feet and is probably the most easily recognized of the poplars. Poplars are a group of trees that generally have light-colored bark and leaves. The leaves possess teeth and are somewhat heart shaped with a point on the end. The teeth vary in size. The cottonwood prefers wet areas, but it is a pioneer tree—one of the first trees to start growing in a field. The cottonwood leaf is triangular with a square base across the bottom; the leaf stem is flattened which makes it wiggle back and forth in the wind. The seed pods produce a prodigious amount of cottonlike fiber, sometimes coating the ground with so much down it looks like snow. In the fall the cottonwood leaves turn a yellowish color. In the winter the tree produces brown, pointed buds.

SHRUBS

Shrubs are small woody plants with multiple stems instead of one main trunk. The leaves can grow anywhere on the stems, from top to bottom. Shrubs vary in height from a couple of feet to well over twenty-five feet. They usually require a certain amount of sunlight to survive, although there are some shrubs that can live in the shade of other trees.

Honeysuckle
page 124

Honeysuckles can be either vines or shrubs depending on the species. They have opposite leaves that are smooth and simple and measure from one to two inches long. The flowers are tubular in shape and the petals are split and curled back at the ends. The blossoms range in color from red to white to yellow, or even yellow and white on the same plant. Honeysuckles produce reddish berries in late summer that are popular with birds.

The name of this plant comes from the honey-like nectar in the blossom. This sweet liquid attracts butterflies, moths, bees, and hummingbirds. Honeysuckles can be found everywhere in the eastern United States.

Wild Rose
page 124

Wild roses have small five-petaled flowers, usually pink. The flowers can be quite small as in the multiflora rose or fairly large (1 1/2 inches across) like those of the pasture rose. Wild roses are related to cultivated roses, but the cultivated varieties have more petals and larger blossoms. Each leaf has three to five leaflets with teeth on them. Rose bushes generally reach two to six feet high and have a great many stems. They have thorns from the base of the stem to the tips of the leaves.

All roses produce fruits called rose hips that look like small apples. The rose hips may or may not be meaty inside. When mature they have a lot of vitamin C. In many places rose hips are used for food such as jellies, jams, and teas. (The apple, a relative of the rose, is actually a type of rose hip.) They are not a preferred bird or animal food, but are sometimes eaten at the end of winter.

Blackberry or Bramble

Bramble is the British term for the blackberry or dewberry bush. The branches have somewhat of a squarish stem and many thorns. The leaves, usually from three to five inches long and very sharply toothed, are attached to the stem near where the thorns are. Blackberry stems are usually green to reddish green and grow anywhere from two to seven feet tall. They usually grow in colonies making a bramble or briar patch, which provides a haven for lots of wildlife. Rabbits eat the bramble stems during the winter. The berries are multiseeded fruits attached to a central stalk. When ripe in midsummer they are purple-black.

Black Raspberry
page 124

Black raspberry is related to the blackberries and has thorny stems with compound leaves. The end leaflet is larger than the leaflets down the leaf stem. The leaflets are toothed. The easiest way to distinguish black raspberries from blackberries is that the black raspberry fruit comes off the stem as a cap and is hollow in the center. In addition, the greenish stem of the black raspberry has a waxy white coating giving it a mildewy look.

Black raspberries can grow five or six feet tall. Leaving a few of these plants on the edge of the yard will produce a summertime treat for you as well as for the animals. The stems can be eaten by rabbits and other critters to sustain them through the winter.

Elderberry
page 124

Elderberry is a shrub that grows up to eight feet tall. It generally prefers a wet habitat and can be found along ditches where there is sufficient moisture. It has white flowers anywhere from six to ten inches across and produces numerous blackish berries. Elderberry leaves are opposite and compound, with five to seven leaflets, and can be up to a foot long. The leaflets have tiny teeth and are also opposite. The stems have warts on them.

Elderberries were used by the pioneers to make spiles for tapping maple trees. A spile is a hollow tube directing the sap from a hole in the tree to the collecting bucket. They used elderberries because the center portion of the stem on the thicker branches is soft, almost cottony, and can be easily

**Elderberry,
continued**

pushed out leaving a hollow tube. Elderberries are generally found in the northwestern part of the eastern United States, though they are often raised horticulturally. The flowers are tasty dipped in pancake batter and fried early in the season. The berries make good wine, syrup, and jelly; in Europe the syrup has been used to control and cure colds.

CHAPTER SEVEN

VINES

Vines are usually woody plants that do not have tall or erect stems. They need support from plants and other objects but are not normally harmful to their support plants.

Climbing or Common Bittersweet
page 125

The vines of the bittersweet can get to be several inches thick and reach heights of fifty to sixty feet, often climbing to the tops of trees. The leaves are alternate, somewhat smooth, and simple. They are shiny and leathery with no teeth along the edge. The bittersweet has a yellowish white flower that blooms early in the springtime. It produces reddish orange berries that when fully ripe break open the outer husk, revealing a bright red berry inside. The vines of the bittersweet are generally smooth and grow in a twisting spiral, often wrapping around branches several times.

The American or native bittersweet has become threatened, so many people are cultivating it in addition to the oriental bittersweet. These plants make a welcome addition to trellises and walls.

Trumpet Vine or Trumpet Creeper
page 125

Trumpet vine grows throughout the eastern United States. The leaves are opposite, compound, and slightly oblong with pronounced teeth. The flowers are up to three inches long and a bright orange or reddish orange in color. It is a spectacular plant for attracting hummingbirds. The vines themselves can grow to be almost shrublike, getting up to five or six feet tall before falling down to the ground again and creeping along. Many times they will climb up poles, buildings, and trees and grow up to fifty feet tall.

Morning Glory
page 125

Morning glories usually do not get as long as other vines, only about ten to fifteen feet. The flower is a long tube with a flared opening called a corolla. It can be blue, white, pink, violet, or deep red. The deep red ones attract hummingbirds. The flowers open during the morning hours and close by midafternoon. The leaves of the morning glory are heart-shaped, smooth, and deeply veined. The vines are thin and twist around almost anything: weeds, shrubs, fences, you name it. They weave nicely in trellises and make a good border. (See also page 222.)

Jimsonweed
page 125

Jimsonweed is a viny plant although it can stand fairly erect by itself. It has a flower similar to that of the morning glory except it is pure white. The flower of the jimsonweed is an slender tube sometimes six to eight inches long. The flower has a tubular green sheath covering it at the bottom. The leaves are deeply lobed or toothed and the seeds are spiny. Jimsonweed is sometimes called loco weed because it causes serious disturbances in animals such as cattle and in humans who eat the plant. It is quite hallucinogenic and even poisonous.

Japanese Honeysuckle
page 125

The Japanese honeysuckle is common throughout the eastern United States. It is probably the easiest vine to grow in our backyard to provide a hedge or a cover along a fence. It also makes an excellent ground cover as it is not able to sustain itself at heights above one foot but can spread across the ground twenty to forty feet. The flowers are yellow and white, about one inch long, and tubular. They are good flowers for hummingbirds because the lips of the tube are split at the end. Honeysuckle leaves are opposite and the vines are smooth and usually a brownish red color. The plant produces a reddish berry that is eaten readily by birds and other animals. If you pluck a flower, pull off the base of the

Japanese Honeysuckle, continued

stem, and pull the stamen through the stem, a tasty drop of nectar will come out. This nectar attracts bees and hummingbirds.

Japanese honeysuckles can escape into the wild and take over many roadsides and forest edges. They cannot tolerate shade and so do not enter forests. They also hybridize readily so there are many different variations of the flowers available. Horticulturally the Japanese honeysuckle is produced in colors other than white and yellow; red is the most sought after.

Wild Cucumber
page 125

Wild cucumber is found over the entire eastern United States, normally in wet areas. The vines can grow up to fifteen to twenty feet. It covers its support with small, twining tendrils that produce white flowers in late summer. The flowers grow in clusters and are under one-half inch long. The leaves of this vine are generally star-shaped similar to cucumber vines. Because its seeds are transferred by birds it can sometimes even be found in a well watered backyard.

The wild cucumber produces a berry or fruit that hangs down from the vine. The fruit is usually between two and three inches long and has large spines up to one-half inch long. If you take off the spines, the fruit is reminiscent of a garden cucumber, although it has very little flesh. Inside there are two to four seeds, larger than pumpkin seeds and similar in color to watermelon seeds (a mottled black and brown). As the season progresses, the fruit dries out and the fibers inside become very netlike, looking almost like a sponge. The bottom of the cucumber opens up and the seeds are reportedly projected as far as twelve to fifteen feet. If dried and stained the cucumber can provide a beautiful, ornate addition to a fall arrangement.

Wild Grape
page 126

The wild grape is found throughout the eastern United States. The vines can grow to be several hun-

Wild Grape,
continued

dred feet long depending on the tree support to which they attach themselves. The base of the vine may be several inches thick. Wild grape vines are generally long-lived, sometimes lasting more than a hundred years. Older grapevines have loose, shredding bark, usually light brown in color. The young vines may be green or brown and are very smooth with tendrils coming from nearly every leaf appendage. The grape leaf is somewhat oval in shape and has teeth on the edges. The leaves can be quite large, ranging from two to eight inches across. The fruits are small, purple, and very heavily seeded. Usually the grapes are less than one-half inch across.

Grapes are usually volunteers in our backyard, their seeds dropped by birds since they are not easily digested. The infant vines then creep to a support and reach upwards to get sunlight. The shoots of the wild grape grow rapidly, sometimes three to six feet during one summer. The branches towards the top of the vine produce the small, bitter grapes after two to three years' growth. During the winter in particular the grapes become an important food crop to overwintering robins, bluebirds, mockingbirds, and cedar waxwings. Other names for the wild grape are fox grape, coon grape, and bitter grape.

Kudzu
page 126

This vine can grow to heights of fifty to eighty feet. Kudzu has a smooth compound leaf with three leaflets. There is sometimes a larger tooth off the middle leaflet somewhat reminiscent of poison ivy. The pinkish purple flower is about one inch long and is somewhat pea-shaped and the vine is quite hairy. It is one of the later plants to start producing leaves and flowers and is a grayish brown for a long time in the spring, blooming late in the summer. The vines can produce roots from which new plants grow.

Kudzu,
continued

Kudzu was introduced into our country as a mechanism to prevent banks from eroding and losing their fertile soils. It grows quite rapidly in the southeastern United States, perhaps as much as fifty to one hundred feet per year, and a small amount of it has moved into the central United States. It is not found in the north. Kudzu has been called the scourge of the south because it overtakes hedgerows, fields, even buildings. It is very difficult to control because the branches, when cut back, get a chance to root again.

Virginia Creeper or Five-leafed Ivy
page 126

Virginia creeper is an ivy that grows in woody areas. Its five leaves have whorled leaflets, tubelike in shape, that arise from the same place on the stem. The leaves can range from three to seven inches in length. The flowers are an inconspicuous green and the berries, similar to the wild grape, hang down in small clusters. The fruits are not edible; some say they are poisonous although many animals eat them. They are not preferred by any species of bird, however, and usually remain on the vines until late in the season. Virginia creeper can grow to a length of several hundred feet. The tendrils that attach themselves to a support have root pads that, like the pads on tree frogs' feet, resemble little suction cups.

Five-leafed ivy is a good border plant; if trimmed back it produces a ground cover that stays approximately fifteen to eighteen inches above the ground. Many people confuse the Virginia creeper with poison ivy, though they are easily distinguishable if you look closely.

The Virginia creeper sometimes does have one or two leaflets missing but all the leaflets arise from the same position on the stem in a whorled arrangement. Poison ivy, on the other hand, has only three leaflets with the terminal leaflet usually set away from the other two. In addition, poison ivy does not have the little suction pads on the tendrils. Poison ivy leaves have large teeth whereas the Virginia creeper sports small teeth that are more or less evenly spaced up and down the oblong leaves.

Poison Ivy
page 126

Poison ivy is found all over the eastern United States. It is a common vine of old fields, backyards, and woods. Poison ivy can grow well over fifty to a hundred feet tall when supported by a large tree. Sometimes it grows as a shrub, getting up to four or five feet on a single stalk; sometimes it climbs a tree and masks the real tree with its own foliage. Poison ivy vines are brown, almost smooth, and have tiny hairs that grasp onto its support. Unlike the Virginia creeper, the hairs do not have suction cups at the end.

Poison ivy leaves have large teeth that sometimes appear lobed, especially on the terminal leaf. The leaves are compound with three leaflets. The center leaflet is generally larger than the other two. A good way to distinguish poison ivy from other three-leaved plants is by the base of the two smaller leaves: there is a reddish or purple-reddish spot where they are attached. The leaflets can be quite varied in size and can grow up to seven or eight inches long. The size depends upon the amount of moisture and the growing conditions of the plant. The leaves are generally a shiny or a glossy green; in the fall they turn reddish. The flowers are small, white or greenish white, and very inconspicuous. The berries produced are white and not edible by humans, although many birds feed on them during the winter, especially the yellow-rumped warbler, mockingbird, and cedar waxwing.

Poison ivy is not a welcome plant in our yards because most people are allergic to it. Touching the vine, stem, or leaves, even during the winter, can cause an extremely itchy rash. Even the smoke from burning plants can bring on a reaction. To get rid of poison ivy you must eradicate it all the way down to the roots. Using hoes and rakes and constantly disturbing the soil will keep it from growing back again.

Bittersweet Nightshade
page 126

Bittersweet nightshade, or deadly nightshade as it is sometimes called, is a common plant along the borders of yards. The vines grow on pine trees, through bushes, and on ornamental trees and shrubs. It grows up to a maximum of ten to twelve feet. The purple flowers are shaped like shooting stars: the five petals curve back and a yellow point comes from the recurved petals. The leaves are generally oblong and range up to three inches in length. At the base of the alternate leaves are two small appendages that look almost like leaflets, though actually they are part of the leaf. The berries hang in groups; they are oblong, bright red, shiny, and approximately one-quarter inch long. Although attractive and tempting, they are extremely poisonous to humans. All the nightshades belong to the tomato, potato, and eggplant family.

Common Nightshade

The common nightshade only gets two to three feet tall and is stalky rather than vinelike. The flowers look very similar to those of the bittersweet nightshade, except the five petals are white as opposed to violet or blue. The berries are black instead of red and are rounder. The leaves are somewhat the same shape as the bittersweet nightshade's except they lack the small side leaves.

Black Nightshade
page 126

The black nightshade is often a serious pest in grain crops where the seeds get transmitted when sowing wheat, barley, corn, and soy beans; farmers often dislike it because the berries stain the grain. It is commonly found in areas with plowed or disturbed soil. The black nightshade has a shiny blue-black berry that hangs down from the stem. These berries are more rounded than the oblong berries of the bittersweet nightshade.

The striking white flowers have petals that curve backwards and hang down. The center part of the flower is a bright yellow. The black nightshade generally is self supporting and rarely grows over three feet tall.

Horse Nettle

Horse nettle is another nightshade we might find in our yards. The plant grows only one or two feet tall. It has spiny stems. The berries are yellowish and up to one-half inch across; they look like small tomatoes. These berries are poisonous and hallucinogenic. It is best not to eat them.

CHAPTER · EIGHT

FLOWERS

The flowers discussed in this chapter are those that are endemic or wild in the eastern United States, though many of them are also cultivated. They are arranged by color: orange, blue and purple, yellow, pink, and white. But be aware that many flowers hybridize, which can cause variations in color.

Many of the flowers included here are perennials, meaning they live more than one season by building up a root stock underground. These require minimal care, much less than do annuals. Many of these perennials produce seed heads that attract wildlife in the fall or that may be harvested and planted the next year. Some people leave the plants through the winter, allowing birds and other animals to feed. This can also be done with annuals.

Some flowers are especially attractive to certain caterpillars and butterflies. Others are planted to attract beneficial insects such as ladybugs and other predator bugs. There are even some plants that emit pheromones, odors, or chemicals that deter insects from coming into the vicinity, especially those that might damage our vegetables or flowers.

· · · · · · **ORANGE FLOWERS** · · · · · ·

Butterfly Weed
page 127

Butterfly weed belongs to the milkweed family. Blooming in early to mid summer, it is bright orange in color and has recurved sepals coming down from the flower. It grows from 1 to 2 1/2 feet tall and produces lancelike leaves. The stems of the butterfly weed are smooth and do not produce milk when broken as milkweeds normally do. The narrow seed pods are similar to milkweed seed pods except they are long and somewhat twisted. They open up in the fall and the flat, round, brown seeds, looking like small ticks attached to parachutes of silk, blow about and reseed themselves. Butterfly weed often attracts butterflies and hummingbirds. If you want to plant it in your garden, get a root stalk from a nursery outlet or garden center.

Orange Hawkweed
page 127

Orange hawkweed is in the sunflower or composite family. A composite has many small, densely clustered flowers. Orange hawkweed is usually not more than one foot tall. The bottom of the plant has a number of leaves arising from one point, making what we call a basal rosette. The basal rosette of leaves shoots up a stalk that bears a composite flower. This flower has a number of petals that are squared off at the end; they are yellowish orange at the center and become brighter orange towards the outside. The hawkweed is a host plant for a number of different insects, especially butterflies. When the flower is finished blooming in early summer, the seeds are very similar to the dandelion's, with fluffy parachutes that carry them from place to place. Like the dandelion, hawkweed comes up in places where it is not planted and not necessarily wanted. It is commonly found in yards that haven't been mowed for quite a while. The orange hawkweed has a relative called the yellow hawkweed. Both can make welcome additions to an unmowed or infrequently mowed portion of a yard. Hawkweed can be found over the entire eastern part of the United States.

Turk's Cap Lily and Day Lily
page 127

The turk's cap lily has orange flowers with black or brown spots on them. The petals are recurved and the stamens and pistils are extremely long with brown at the end. The leaves are whorled—they originate from the same point on the stem. The plant may grow from two to four feet tall. A wild plant similar to this is the day lily. The day lily has linear leaves anywhere from one to two feet long arising from the bottom of the plant. The flower does not have brown spots on it but does have somewhat recurved petals. Day lilies can be found growing in wild areas that are not maintained by mowing or cultivation. A number of the wild orange lilies, like the Canada lily, tiger lily, Michigan lily, and wood lily, are protected and endangered, so it is best not to pick or to dig any in a natural area.

• • • • BLUE AND PURPLE FLOWERS • • • •

Wild Chicory
page 127

Wild chicory can be found over the entire eastern United States usually growing along roadsides, pasture lands, and areas presently uncultivated. They grow anywhere from two to six feet tall. These striking blue flowers are composites. They do not do well in full direct sunlight and usually bloom early in the morning, closing up as afternoon progresses. Chicory has a basal rosette of leaves, though not as dramatic as that of the hawkweeds, and the petals are squared off at the ends. The stems are stiff and smooth with a zigzag growth pattern; as each flower is formed it causes a change of direction in the stem. The blue blossoms are attached directly to the stem as if they were glued onto it. It is probably the most common late summertime plant found along roadways. Occasionally chicory flowers will be white.

Dried and ground chicory roots can be used as a coffee substitute. Some types of chicory have been cultivated to produce a blend to mix with coffee when coffee is extremely expensive.

Periwinkle
page 127

Periwinkle, also called myrtle, is quite a common ground cover all over the eastern United States. It has small, five-petaled blue flowers that look like little pinwheels. Periwinkle has shiny opposite leaves about 1 to 1 1/4 inches long. The length of the plant as it grows along the ground can be several feet, but it only gets about a foot above the ground. As the stem crawls along, it puts out additional roots that we call *adventitious roots*; they send up tall stalks that produce the flowers. Periwinkle makes a thick ground cover, crowding out weeds and other wildflowers. It likes rich soil and is somewhat resistant to shade.

Blue Violet
page 127

The blue or purple violet has heart-shaped leaves, usually grows somewhere between six and ten inches from the ground, and has five-petaled flowers. There are generally two petals somewhat close together at the top of the flower, two petals coming out almost at right angles to the center, and one larger petal coming down from the bottom. A drop of nectar is found on the pointed or base end of the flower and attracts insects. Most often the center of the flower is a very light color from yellow to white. They appear in early springtime.

Violets produce a seed capsule towards the bottom of the plant, where another group of flowers grows. The capsules are somewhat triangular in shape and as the season progresses they dry and gain tension on the outer walls. When completely dry they pop open and shoot the seeds a good distance, sometimes twelve to fifteen feet. Picking the flower does not seem to damage the reproductive capability of a violet.

Ground Ivy or Gill-over-the-ground
page 127

Gill-over-the-ground is a small variety of mint growing along the ground. The vine or stem often reaches two or three feet long, although the erect part doesn't get higher than eight or ten inches. Gill-over-the-ground has a square stem; the leaves of this plant, about one inch across, are roundish with deeply scalloped teeth. The tiny blue flowers rise in the midst of the leaves. The flower is tubular and somewhat orchidlike with petals of various sizes. The bottom petals curve downward, often separating into two or three lobes.

Gill-over-the-ground can withstand extensive mowing and chopping. It tends to grow in wet soil and blooms all summer.

Bird's-eye Speedwell
page 127

Speedwells are tiny plants that creep across the ground similar to gill-over-the-ground. The leaves and stem have downy hair covering them. The leaves are heart-shaped with large teeth. The vines normally get only about one foot long, though the vines with flowers grow a little bit longer. Speedwell, also known as veronica, belongs to the snapdragon family so the flowers are somewhat tubular; they have four petals and the bottom petal usually hangs down. It is used as a border plant. Bird's-eye speedwell, one of the more common varieties, can be found throughout the eastern United States.

Cow Vetch
page 127

The cow vetch, a member of the pea family, may have either blue or pink flowers. It is described in the pink flower section along with crown vetch.

• • • • • YELLOW FLOWERS • • • • •

Buttercup
page 128

The buttercup is an easy flower to identify. It has five and sometimes up to seven yellow petals that are glossy or shiny. The flower head is approximately one-half inch across. The plant may range in size from a few inches to a couple of feet tall. The leaves are palmate and deeply cut, much like celery leaves. Buttercups normally grow in rich soil that is a little moist. They bloom May through June and can be found over the entire eastern United States.

Celandine
page 128

The celandine has four bright yellow petals. The leaves usually have five lobes with rounded teeth on them, rather like an oak leaf. It usually grows in wooded areas and reaches eight to twenty-four inches in height. This plant can be found over the entire eastern United States especially in rich, old forest soils.

Common Purslane
page 128

Purslanes do not usually get more than one foot tall. They have small paddle- or heart-shaped leaves and tiny yellow flowers. The flowers normally have five petals. The leaves are somewhat reminiscent of cactus leaves as they are rather thick at the base. Often the leaves seem to arise from the same position on the stem, giving them a rosette appearance. Purslanes can be found over almost the entire eastern United States especially in areas where the soil has been disturbed or in a garden that has lain fallow for half a season.

St. Johnswort
page 128

St. Johnswort is a summertime flower with five yellow petals. It grows over the entire eastern United States in weedy areas that have not been mown or cultivated for a season. It normally grows from five to fifteen inches tall, though it can reach up to almost three feet. The leaves are opposite, somewhat lance-shaped, and smooth-edged. If you hold the leaves up to the sunlight you will see some translucent dots that look like little eyeglass lenses. Sometimes these dots are a bit oblong. When dried the St. Johnswort seed heads make a nice dried flower addition to a winter bouquet.

Flower-of-an-hour
page 128

This pale five-petaled flower can be found through much of the eastern United States except the extreme north. The leaves are alternate and three-lobed; the lobes are very thin and have rounded teeth like those of a white oak leaf. The easiest way to identify this flower is to look for the five pale yellow petals and a purple color in the center. The flower-of-an-hour is a weedy species usually found in areas where the soil has been disturbed in the past but is not presently being cultivated.

Black Mustard or Yellow Rocket
page 128

The mustards are found throughout the entire eastern United States. The black mustard or yellow rocket has a height of about two to three feet. Like all the mustards the flower has four yellow petals. The leaves are rather oblong in shape and are

Black Mustard
or Yellow Rocket,
continued

deeply lobed and cut with secondary teeth. The upper leaves of the black mustard, however, are not as finely lobed and cut as the lower leaves. The mustard family has characteristic seed pods that look like small hot dogs or small bean or pea pods. Mustard usually thrives in areas that are gardened but left fallow for a short time and may pop up in a yard that is not mown frequently.

Sedum, Mossy Stonecrop, or Wall Pepper
page 128

This plant is fairly small, only two to six inches. It usually grows in large clumps called beds or mats. The sedums are low-growing plants that often grow on rocks, cliffs, and walls. The name wall pepper comes from the peppery taste of the leaves. The leaves are quite small, usually under one-quarter inch long, and grow close to the stem. The flowers usually bloom during the early part of the summer. Some sedums can have red, pink, or white flowers. The five petals of the stonecrop are reminiscent of stars. Stonecrop is seldom found in our yard except where we plant rock gardens, but it does grow wild in the northern parts of North America, especially in rocky and wooded areas.

Five Finger or Cinquefoil
page 128

The five finger or cinquefoil has yellow flowers with five petals. The compound leaves, which are deeply toothed, usually have five leaflets, but sometimes seven to nine. It can grow just a few inches tall or up to two or three feet. In spite of its resemblance to the marijuana plant, cinquefoil has no hallucinogenic properties. Cinquefoil can be found over the entire eastern United States. It will grow in most any situation: in a rock garden, in our yards, and in cultivated areas. There is also a shrubby cinquefoil that is grown ornamentally. Most cinquefoils bloom during the summer.

Bird's-foot Trefoil
page 128

Bird's-foot trefoil grows over the entire eastern United States along the edges of our yards where we have not mown for quite a while. It can grow to heights of about one foot or more. The flowers are similar to a snapdragon, with a large lobe over a smaller lobe. The compound leaves are rather small and the three leaflets are bunched together at the end in a shamrocklike arrangement. Bird's-foot trefoil is a very pretty flower, especially in sandy soils.

Yellow Wood Sorrel
page 128

Yellow wood sorrel does not get very tall; instead it creeps across the ground. The easiest way to identify this plant is by the five yellow petals and the shamrocklike leaves, which have three heart-shaped lobes. Wood sorrel blooms during much of the summer though it usually is not found in full sunlight. It grows all over the eastern United States.

Virginia Ground Cherry
page 129

The ground cherries have bell-like flowers; the bells are fairly shallow, not long like the trumpet creeper or morning glory. There are some purplish spots on the yellow petals. Both the Virginia ground cherry and the smooth ground cherry have oblong leaves with small teeth. The leaf is fairly long, arrow-shaped, and opposite, and the flowers hang from a short stem. The yellow cherrylike fruit has a sheath around it, which gives it a Chinese lantern look. (Another name for this plant is the Chinese lantern.) Ground cherries grow up to about three feet. In the wild they prefer rich, well drained soils.

Black-eyed Susan
page 129

The black-eyed Susan is one of the composite flowers: the actual flower is in the center and the outer petals are used to attract pollinating insects. It has multiple yellow petals with a dark brown eye or flower head in the center. The leaves are long and slender; often they have hairs or bristles that give them a fuzzy look. The black-eyed Susan can grow

grow from 1 to 3½ feet tall. It is found in dry fields, yards, and open meadows throughout the eastern United States.

Dandelion
page 129

The dandelion is a composite flower. It has a bright head of yellow petals that are squarish at the end. The leaf is long and slender with huge teeth that point downward, cutting into the leaf. One of the first flowers to bloom in the spring, dandelions hold their heads quite erect. They can be short, only a couple of inches high, or they can grow up to eighteen inches in an open field. The flower head turns into a white golf ball-size bunch of seeds that float about like tiny parachutes. When broken, the stem and leaf of the dandelion exude a milky substance.

The dandelion grows anyplace there is disturbed soil that is not mown too low. This perennial is very difficult to get rid of except by destroying it with herbicides or digging up the long roots. The seeds are a favorite of birds, especially goldfinches, indigo buntings, and sparrows. The leaves can be used for salad greens in the springtime before they get bitter. A very mild white wine can be made from the flowers.

Yellow Goatsbeard
page 129

Goatsbeard produces a flower similar to the dandelion and also similar to the orange hawkweed. It has the habit of folding up its flowers during the afternoon hours. It is a very tall plant, reaching over three feet high. The leaves are smooth and quite long, and clasp the stem. The seed head is very similar to the dandelion's except it is larger, about 2½ inches across. The yellow goatsbeard is a weedy species usually found along roadsides and vacant fields in all the eastern states. Like the dandelion it produces a milky substance when cut or broken.

Yellow Hawkweed
page 129

The yellow hawkweeds have composite flowers similar to those of dandelion and orange hawkweed. The most characteristic feature is the squared-off petals. Yellow hawkweed usually has a basal rosette of leaves that are long and slender. The leaves are sometimes hairy and are not toothed. Hawkweeds produce a tiny puff of seed heads very similar to dandelions. Generally the yellow hawkweeds are from 1 to 2^1/$_2$ feet tall, though some can get taller. They are found over the entire eastern United States. They normally grow in soil that has been left fallow for more than a year.

Common Tansy
page 129

Common tansy is a composite and belongs to the daisy family. It has small buttonlike flowers that are gathered at the top of the plant and occasionally on the ends of side branches. These flowers are quite dense and are a very bright yellow; they look similar to the center of a daisy. The leaves are quite dissected, almost fernlike, like those of the Queen Anne's lace. They grow up to 4^1/$_2$ or 5 feet tall, usually along roadsides where there is good drainage, and can be found all over the eastern United States. Tansy is a very aromatic plant. It is lovely in dried flower arrangements because the flower buttons remain intact for years.

Moth Mullein
page 129

The moth mullein belongs to the snapdragon family and can be found throughout the eastern part of the United States. The leaves grow mostly at the bottom of the stem; the stalk has very few. The five-petaled flower can be a variety of colors: yellow, white, and sometimes pink. The anthers are bright orange and the stamens are purple. Moth mulleins like to grow where there is open sunlight, usually in lawns and fields that have not been recently mown. The moth mullein is a biennial so it takes two years to grow. The first year it just a basal rosette of leaves.

Bouncing Bet
page 130

Bouncing bet belongs to the campion family. It has five petals that are the end of a tube or calyx. The leaves are paired. It usually is not more than 1 1/2 to 2 feet tall. Bouncing bet blooms a long time during early summer. This plant is also called soapwort because if you take the flowers in your hand with a bit of water and rub your hands vigorously, you will get soapsuds. Bouncing bet generally grows in colonies numbering from four or five plants to well over a hundred. It is one of the plants that invades sand dunes as a stabilizing agent. It grows over the entire eastern United States, especially where the land is fairly well drained.

Deptford Pink
page 130

Deptford pink has five petals that, as in the bouncing bet, are the extension of the calyx. It usually reaches no more than eighteen inches high. The flower is quite small, about one-half inch across. It is a very delicate pink and the center is an even lighter pink. Often there are little spots of white on the petals. The leaves are long and slender, very similar to grass, and they clasp the stem at the base of the leaf. Deptford pink can be found throughout the eastern United States where there is a bit of dry land.

Corn Cockle
page 130

The corn cockle has the same flower arrangement: five petals coming from a calyx or tube, except the petals are bent backward and are quite wide giving it an almost roselike appearance. The sepals extend out beyond the petals and make the blossom look star-shaped. It is a slender plant with grasslike leaves. The corn cockle can get up to three feet tall and is found in well drained areas over the entire eastern United States.

Rose Moss or Moss Pink
page 131

Rose moss belongs to the phlox family, which has a long calyx or tube ending in five petals. The petals of the flower are scalloped. The leaves are slender, needlelike, and whorled around the stem. It grows to a height of about six inches. It is found mainly in the northern half of the eastern United States; sometimes it is transplanted into gardens in other areas, especially in the south.

Pennsylvania Smartweed or Pink Knotweed
page 131

The knotweeds have tiny pink flowers that grow in clusters. These can be found at the end of the stems and at the leaf axils. They belong to the buckwheat family. The knotweeds can grow to a height of six feet but are generally from two to three feet. Their name comes from the large knot formed where the leaf clasps the stem. The leaves are alternate. It can be found in any weedy areas throughout the United States; some even grow in water. The Pennsylvania smartweed has hairy stems and the leaves are slender and smooth.

Musk Mallow
page 130

Musk mallow reaches about two feet in height. The flower head is about 1 to 1 1/2 inches across. It has five petals that are deeply notched at the end and can be either pink or white. The center of the flower has a large column of stamens that protrude from the center. The leaves are maple-leaf shape but with very narrow lobes. It is found over the entire eastern United States. It usually grows in well drained soil at the edges of yards.

Dame's Rocket
page 131

Dame's rocket is one of the mustards and has four petals. Though its coloring is similar to phlox, the two are easily distinguished because phlox has five petals. The flowers are all clustered at the top. The seed pod is long and quite pointed. The leaves are pointed at the end and have teeth. The dame's rocket is often planted in cemeteries because it grows well on its own without much care. It reaches one to three feet tall and is usually found in clusters of anywhere from four or five plants to several hundred. The flower can also be purple or white and is sometimes called dame's violet.

Clover
page 131

The clovers belong to the pea family. Their blossoms are very tiny and clustered together at the end of the plant, usually in a flower head. It generally has five petals for each minute flower, with the bottom two petals fused together. The two side petals make winglike appendages and the top one bends down over the rest. Clover leaves usually come in threes and are compound. The leaf often has different colorations in it such as purples and deep greens.

Clovers can get fairly high, growing from one to three feet. They are found throughout the eastern United States wherever there is well drained soil. The small clovers especially are beneficial in our yards because they add nitrogen to the soil and help thicken the yard mat. The larger clovers with the big flowers are a good source of food for rabbits and mice. Some birds eat the seed heads in the wintertime. Although most of the clovers have pink flowers there are some that can be white, particularly the smaller varieties, or lavender.

Dogbane or Spreading Dogbane
page 130

The spreading dogbane normally grows in a wooded area and seldom in the open sunlight. It has tiny bright pink flowers that hang down like little bells with five recurved petals. These flowers are usually not much bigger than one-quarter to one-half inch long. The plant is very similar to and frequently confused with milkweed. As with milkweed, when the stem is broken dogbane will exude a milky juice. The leaves are opposite, oval in shape, and smooth-edged. The seed pods are long and needlelike, reminiscent of very thin milkweed pods or thin coffee bean pods.

The name dogbane probably comes from the plant's tendency to grow so thickly that a dog would have great difficulty making its way through. The name may also have originated from the plant's poisonous qualities.

Common Morning Glory
page 125

The morning glory is a vinelike plant that can be found along the edges of our yards, in fence rows, and along roadsides. It has a large flower anywhere from two to three inches long and about $1\,1/2$ to 2 inches across. It can be pink, white, or blue. The leaves are smooth, very broad, and heart-shaped, similar to those of a violet. The vines can climb up to ten or fifteen feet into trees and shrubs or on fence rows. They can also crawl across the ground if there is nothing to climb on. Morning glories make a good cover plant for hedges and walls. The pink variety is often frequented by hummingbirds as a source of nectar; many butterflies and moths also like the morning glory. It can be found anyplace in the United States. (See also page 202.)

Peppermint
page 130

The peppermints or spearmints are in the mint family. They are widespread and can be found throughout the eastern United States. Characteristic of mints, the small flowers have a lip hanging down and a hood over the top, rather like orchids. They also have a long tube similar to some of the morning glories. The flowers can be a variety of colors including pink, white, red, purple, and blue. The stems are square and most of the plants are very aromatic. The leaves are toothed and usually opposite; the flowers originate at the upper part of the plant at the leaf axis. They grow readily in rich soil if watered often. Most of the mints do not get very tall, from six inches to two feet.

Daisy Fleabane
page 131

The fleabane is an aster. (White asters are discussed in the white flower section.) The daisy fleabane is a composite that grows along the edges of yards throughout the eastern United States. The flower can be pink or white. It is one of the first asters to bloom in the springtime.

Spotted Knapweed
page 131

The knapweeds are in the composite family with the dandelions, asters, and daisies. The spotted knapweed grows in dry soil. The flower head is compound with all the petals coming out from a central stem. Underneath the petals is a bulbous projection that looks like a small pineapple. Spotted knapweed leaves are deeply cut with fingerlike indentations. The leaves are fairly thin. The plant is tall and wiry and grows to about $2^1/2$ feet.

Bull Thistle or Pasture Thistle
page 131

The bull thistles are quite easily recognized: they are almost the only plants that have spines on both the leaves and stem. They grow in well cultivated and well drained areas. The flower heads are bright pink and composite and arise from a bulb-shaped projection that also has spines on it. When the bull thistle matures it produces cottony seeds that many birds use for nesting material, especially the goldfinch. Pasture thistles can grow up to four or five feet tall. They are found throughout the eastern United States.

Cow Vetch and Crown Vetch
pages 127 and 131

Both the cow vetch and crown vetch are in the pea family so they have the characteristic pealike flower: two petals fused at the bottom, two sticking out from the side, and a hood over the top. Both can be found throughout the eastern United States. They have compound leaves that are pinnate, which means the leaflets are opposite each other and the leaves alternate on the stem.

Cow Vetch and Crown Vetch, continued

The cow vetch is more of a vine. Its flowers grow in a line down the tendril whereas the crown vetch's flowers are clustered at the tip of the plant. The cow vetch does not flower as abundantly as the crown vetch and is often grown for hay and food for cattle. The crown vetch has been planted extensively along roadsides to control erosion and in some areas has become quite a pest. It can grow to two feet tall, whereas the cow vetch can reach heights of two and three feet. Both produce seed pods that look like small bean or pea pods. As these pods mature and dry out, they pop open and scatter the seeds to the ground. Both of these plants add nitrogen to the soil.

Wild Rose
page 130

The rose, also included in the shrub section (see page 198), is a thorn-bearing bush in which animals can take refuge. Wild roses generally have five petals on their pink flowers. The stems have thorns on them and can grow up to six or seven feet tall. The leaves are compound and have three, five, or seven leaflets. The flowers produce a round red or orange fruit called the rose hip; the flower end of this fruit will have vestiges of the five petals, making it almost apple-shaped at the end. At the end of winter they become a very good survival food. Wild roses usually appear in your yard because bird droppings contained some rose seeds.

• • • • • • • WHITE FLOWERS • • • • • • •

Pokeweed
page 132

Pokeweed or pokeberry is an easy plant to identify. The stems are quite red and the flowers are white and hang in clusters like grapes. The flowers are never much more than one-quarter inch across. There can be anywhere from thirty to fifty flowers per bunch. The plant grows quite rapidly, usually up to five or six feet; with good support it can grow eight to ten feet tall.

**Pokeweed,
continued**

As the pokeweed matures it becomes poisonous to humans, especially the roots and berries. The small, purple, pumpkin-shaped berries are eaten by birds and other animals, though they do not last very long. The smell of squashed pokeberries is an acrid, musty odor and one you won't soon forget. Pokeweed is found through much of the eastern United States except for the extreme northern part of Michigan and the east coast from northern Pennsylvania to Maine.

White Campion
page 132

White campion, snowy campion, and catchfly are all common names for the same flower. The flowers have five petals and a bladder-shaped projection behind the blossom where the reproductive body is found. The bladder can be round or very narrow and tubular. This plant gets the name catchfly or bladder campion because of the myth (completely untrue) that flies crawl inside the bladder and are caught and eaten by the flower. The white campion has opposite leaves that are two to three inches long, slender, and smooth. It grows in any undisturbed area that has been reclaimed from cultivation, such as old fields and meadows, and is common all over the United States.

The evening lychnis is probably the most common of the white campions and the first to come out in the spring. When dried, the seeds of the evening lychnis can make a fine addition to a dried flower arrangement.

Queen Anne's Lace or Wild Carrot
page 132

Queen Anne's lace is probably the most familiar white flower in our backyards and neighborhoods. It can grow to a height of two or three feet. The flowers are flat-topped and anywhere from two to five inches across. They are actually a composite of hundreds of tiny flowers. In the center of the flower head there is often a small black or purple flower. This might imitate an insect and induce other

Queen Anne's Lace, continued

insects to land on the flower, thereby insuring that pollen is carried from one flower to another. Studies have shown that plants with the purple flowers do have a higher percentage of fertilization.

The Queen Anne's lace is a biennial: it takes two years for it to produce a flower head. The first year it grows a lacy, dissected carrotlike leaf, takes in energy, and develops a large root stock. This root stock provides the energy for the flower head the following year. It is quite persistent when chopped down, especially in its second year when it produces two or three flower heads. Queen Anne's lace, if dried properly, is beautiful in dried flower arrangements. When it dries naturally in the field the flower head cups itself and looks like a bird nest.

Queen Anne's lace is called wild carrot because it belongs to the carrot family. Our domestic carrot is said to be a direct descendant of the Queen Anne's lace. If you take the roots out of the ground, especially in the first year, they are edible although quite bitter.

Field Bindweed
page 132

Field bindweed, a tube-shaped flower, is actually a morning glory that grows wild in fields. The field bindweed is a little smaller than our common morning glory. It creeps across the ground and winds its stem around obstacles. The white flowers are no more than two inches across and two inches deep. The leaves are much longer than morning glory leaves and are shaped like arrowheads. The field bindweed is an annual plant. The seeds are carried by birds and they can remain in a bird's digestive tract for quite a long time.

White Aster
page 132

White aster is probably the most common aster; there are fifty different varieties found in our yards and neighborhoods. White asters are composites with a tremendous number of tiny flowers radiating from one head. This is the same kind of flower head

**White Aster,
continued**

you would find on a dandelion or a hawkweed. The centers usually are yellow and the petals are white. The petals attract pollinating insects to the center where the actual flowers are found. Generally the leaves are toothed and slender and are in varying sizes. A white aster found in the woods would have a wider leaf.

White asters can be one to four feet high. They are usually found in fields that have been fallow for a while. For the most part they are perennials, growing up from the root stocks of past years. Most white asters bloom in late summer and fall. The daisy fleabane is the first white aster to bloom in the spring, usually by late May or early June. Supposedly rubbing the flowers and leaves of this plant on your dog will keep it from getting fleas.

White Daisy or Oxeye Daisy
page 132

An oxeye daisy is a white flower with an extremely bright yellow center. The flowers are usually about two inches across and have a small indent in the center. The leaves are long and deeply lobed, reminiscent of oak leaves. The plant normally grows from one to three feet tall. Oxeye daisies are found over most of the United States along roadsides and barren fields where the ground tends to be dry. Many of the ornamental daisies that we grow in our yards are descendants of the oxeye daisy. Unlike many wildflowers it is very hardy and can last a long time in a flower arrangement.

Virginia Waterleaf
page 132

The Virginia waterleaf has a tubular flower that is approximately one-half inch long with five lobes at the end. The leaves are heavily dissected, somewhat like maple leaves. In the early spring when the leaves emerge they are blotched with white as if water had dripped on them and left a lime spot. As the plant matures during the summer this spot becomes less evident. Waterleaf, sometimes called Miami mist, is tolerant of shade but can also live in open sunlight. It likes moist soil that is fairly rich. Many people plant a type of waterleaf called phacelia to enhance the borders of their yards.

Yarrow
page 132

Yarrow is a flat-topped flower somewhat like the Queen Anne's lace. The leaves are smaller than the wild carrot's and more dissected or lacy, but are similar in shape. The flowers on the top have an umbrel and each tiny flower has five white petals. It belongs to the composite family and is a biennial, taking two years to produce a flower.

The yarrow can be found throughout the eastern United States where the ground has been left fallow for a short time. It grows in clumps up to three feet tall. The plant is quite aromatic; another name for yarrow is sneezeweed. The leaves were used as gauze on wounds in World War I. When picked at its peak and dried upside down, yarrow can be dyed for dried flower arrangements. Perennial yarrows have been cultivated in different colors from gold to pink to purple.

WEEDS WITH TINY FLOWERS

Weeds have two definitions. The first and most common is a plant that is not wanted. The real definition, however, is a plant that is adapted to man's disturbance of the soil.

Many of the weeds in our yards have small, inconspicuous flowers, usually green. These plants grow and produce seeds quickly so the flowers are short-lived, but they can be quite pretty. Take some time to look at these plants when you locate them in your yard.

Flowering Spurge
page 133

Flowering spurge has tiny flowers with five white petals at the very tip of the plant. The whorled leaves begin at the same place that the flower bracts do. Below that point the stem has alternate leaves that are long and lancelike, growing up to about $2^1/2$ inches long. The plant itself can grow to be three feet. When the stem of the flowering spurge is broken it is spindly unlike a milkweed, but it does exude a milky substance. This plant is found in the northern half of the eastern United States from Indiana, Ohio, and Pennsylvania northward.

Chickweed
page 133

Chickweed has five white petals so deeply cleft they look like ten petals. The sepals are usually longer than the petals. You can also see the pronounced anthers coming out from the center of the flower, looking like dots of pepper against the white petals. The common chickweed grows quite rapidly, creeping across the ground up to two feet in length. It has smooth, oval leaves that are opposite on the stem.

Lamb's-quarters
page 133

Lamb's-quarters has a flower that is green, quite small, and usually located right above a leaf bract close to the stem. It is very easy to overlook. The flowers quickly turn into a green seed. Lamb's-quarters is an annual plant that grows in highly cultivated areas; it is probably the most common plant to come up in your vegetable and flower gardens. The leaf is diamond or triangular in shape with obvious teeth. The underside is a light gray or light green. As the seeds are ripening, usually in late summer and early fall, they may develop a maroon or reddish cast. This plant is found throughout the eastern United States.

Horehound

Horehound, also called water horehound or bugleweed, is one of the mints. It has a square stem and opposite toothed leaves that are approximately two inches long; it reaches about two feet in height. The small white flowers are clustered in groups around the base of the leaves, as in most of the mints. The horehound is different from other mints in that the leaves and stems do not give off an odor. It generally grows in moist areas in the northern tier of states across eastern North America.

Galium or Bedstraw
page 133

Galium, also called bedstraw because pioneers reputedly used it to fill their mattresses, is quite a common plant in both wooded and open areas. It has small white or greenish white flowers with four petals. The leaves are usually small, whorled, and clustered around the stem. They are short and thin, lancelike in shape, and have no teeth. The stem may be smooth or have hairs with tiny hooks. Bedstraw can spread across the ground or grow somewhat erect up to about one foot in height. In recently cultivated areas the plants can make a dense mat of greenery. The tiny hooks or hairs on the stems hold the mats together. Galium can be found over the entire eastern United States.

Carpetweed
page 133

Carpetweed, also called sea purslane, is a plant that creeps along the ground. It has oval leaves, a long stem, and tubular flowers. The petals of the flowers are either absent or fused at the axis of the leaves and are very tiny, not easily noticed. Usually carpet weed is found in coastal or sandy areas in the eastern part of the United States; it is almost absent from the Midwest.

Shepherd's Purse
page 133

Shepherd's purse, one of the mustards, can grow to be about two feet tall. The leaves at the base of the plant are deeply cut and toothed, somewhat like dandelion leaves. At the top of the plant the leaves are lancelike or long and tubular with some teeth. The tiny white flowers grow at the very tip of the plant. The most obvious characteristic of the shepherd's purse is its seed pod, which forms as the flower matures. It is in the shape of a heart and looks similar to the sheep bladders shepherds utilized as purses. When dried, the pods can be used in flower arrangements. Because it is a mustard the seed pods are edible and have a little bite to them. It can be found over the entire eastern United States.

Purple Dead Nettle
page 133

The purple dead nettle or red dead nettle belongs to the mint family and has square stems. The tiny orchidlike blossoms are usually at the axis of the leaves close to the stem. The purple dead nettle doesn't get very tall—generally less than a foot and most often under six inches. The upper leaves can become purplish giving the overall plant a flower-like look. The leaves are very close together, often overlapping each other and hiding the flowers underneath. Like all the mints, the dead nettle is aromatic. It can be found throughout the eastern United States, especially in areas that haven't been disturbed for a couple of years.

Common Plantain
page 133

Common plantain has extremely small white flowers. Looking at them from a standing position, they appear to be long green spikes coming from wide leaves on the ground. Very rarely do they get to be more than one foot tall. The leaves lie flat and are egg-shaped with some serration along the edges.

Common plantain does well in disturbed soils. It has been said that plantains work well as poultices for wounds. The seeds are good bird food.

Buckhorn Plantain
page 133

A relative of the common plantain can also be found in our yards. This is the English or buckhorn plantain, sometimes called white man's footprint because it is so adaptable to cultivation. The curved stems of the buckhorn plantain leaves become reddish towards the base. These leaves are long and thin. Both buckhorn and common plantain can be found over the entire eastern United States.

Buckhorn is the most common weed in our lawns. It is so persistent that mowing slows it down only a little. Within a day the plant will shoot up another flower spike.

GRASSES

Grasses are small plants generally ranging from just a few inches tall to four and five feet tall. The longer ones are the native prairie grasses. Grasses traditionally have hollow stems and long linear leaves that clasp the stems much as an apron wraps around a person. The end of the stem has the flower head that produces seeds. The seeds generally are wind pollinated or scattered by hooking onto animals. Grass seeds live a long time in the soil and can start growing anytime we allow disturbed soil to remain fallow.

Because the identifying characteristics of grasses usually only develop when the grass grows tall, the descriptions here won't always help identify the grass of a lawn.

Bermuda Grass
page 134

Bermuda grass is a low-growing grass. It can creep along the surface of the ground and produce many plants, growing up to four or five feet long. Bermuda grass propagates itself by sending runners along the ground, which then shoot stems into the air that produce seeds. The seed head has long spikes somewhat reminiscent of straight octopus arms. The seeds grow on the sides of the spikes and look like tiny yellowish peanuts. The leaves extend sideways from the stem, almost perpendicular to it. Bermuda grass is fairly tolerant of dry, hot weather. In the northern part of the United States, tilling the soil in the fall will kill the plant by exposing it to the cold.

Crabgrass
page 134

Crabgrass looks similar to Bermuda grass, though the leaves of the crabgrass are wider. The flower heads stand fairly erect. Crabgrass normally starts growing in early summer as it needs warmer soil. It grows in tufts and clumps that originate from a single root stock. It is an annual grass and must start from seeds every year. Once the grass has started to grow it is difficult to control; pieces of stems and roots alone will start a new colony of grass. Pulling the crabgrass and tilling the soil are the most effective ways of controlling it. Crabgrass cannot sustain competition from other perennial grasses that might be in our lawns, so keeping the lawn relatively tall and well mowed will prevent the crabgrass from taking over. Crabgrass can be found over the entire United States.

Goose Grass
page 134

Goose grass is sometimes called crowfoot because the seed head looks like the toes of a crow. The "toes" are thick and radiate out from the tips of the stems a distance of one to two inches. Goose grass is somewhat similar to quack grass except the goose grass seed head is thicker and the leaves are thicker and heavier. The seeds are brown and wheat-shaped, and they have small dark stripes on them.

Goose grass is found mainly in the southern part of eastern United States where it grows in lawns and gardens, sometimes taking over old fields. It likes to grow in pathways and walkways in soil that is compacted. It is usually spread about in singular plants. Mowing and cultivating usually gets rid of the goose grass. Birds and other animals readily eat the seeds.

Quack Grass
page 134

Quack grass, found throughout the eastern United States, grows across the ground rather like crabgrass, although not as prolific. The stems shoot straight up and produce fairly large leaves, sometimes up to three feet high. An identifying feature of quack grass is the seed stalk, which has a zigzag pattern of seeds. The stem even twists in a zigzag.

Quack grass can invade our yards and gardens. Mowing the lawn will help control the quack grass population and eventually eradicate it. Any portion of the stem that is broken off can produce a new plant. Quack grass can be persistent on walls and in rock gardens. The roots and the underground stems clasp onto the sides of the rocks, making control of this plant very difficult.

Timothy
page 134

Timothy grass grows from 2¹/₂ to 3 feet tall. It normally gets into waste areas that are not cultivated or mowed; it is not common in maintained gardens or lawns. Timothy can be recognized by its tall flower and seed stalk. The small flower head looks like a long cattail or a long hot dog.

Timothy is good to plant in old fields because it provides lots of nutrients for the soil. It has been used extensively as a forage crop for cattle and horses and can also be used to stabilize hillsides where erosion is a problem.

Kentucky Bluegrass
page 134

Kentucky bluegrass is probably the most common grass in the United States because it is frequently grown in our lawns. Although not often seen with its flower head, when mown Kentucky bluegrass provides a rich mat of leaves, giving us luscious green lawns. The leaves are wide and fairly short; they become quite thick at the base of the plant. If allowed to grow to maturity the Kentucky bluegrass can get to be about three feet high; the flower spike and the seed spike extend another four or five inches. The seed spikes radiate from the center stem and produce seeds on little side branches. Kentucky bluegrass is often used as a pasture grass for horses in the southern United States.

Tall Redtop
page 134

Tall redtop can be found over most of the eastern United States. It is a tall grass, two to three feet high, with very narrow leaves. The seed heads are feathery and have little stalks radiating out at the very tip of the plant from which the seeds hang. The seeds look like tiny orange grains of wheat. The grass gets the name tall redtop because in the late summer the seeds and flowers become reddish or purplish in color. This is especially apparent in a dense mat of plants—it gives an overall purplish cast to the countryside.

The tall redtop is not a palatable plant for livestock. It can pop up in yards and gardens where there is disturbed soil. Tilling the soil is probably the best way to get rid of the tall redtop. It cannot withstand a lot of cultivation.

Orchard Grass
page 134

Orchard grass grows all over the eastern United States. Its leaves are relatively wide but do not grow very tall. It has very thick stems. The fruiting stem is at the end of the plant, and as the ripe side stems open and show more than one seed pod, it takes on a thick, mustachelike appearance. Orchard grass blooms in late May or June and gets to be about $2^1/_2$ to 5 feet tall.

Foxtail Grass

Foxtails are found over the entire eastern United States, especially where land has lain fallow for a while. The seed head is bushy at the end, much like a fox's tail, and frequently droops over to one side. Foxtail grass, also called bristle grass, grows from one to three feet high. It provides a good source of seeds in the early fall and winter because it stays above the ground. Both the foxtail and orchard grass have rather stiff stems and do not get knocked down by winter storms and snow as early as the other grasses.

CHAPTER · TEN

FERNS, MOSSES, AND FUNGI

When we are out and about our yards, we frequently come across plants that are not easily put in one group or another. These include ferns, mosses, liverworts, lichens, fungi, and slime molds. Most are quite small and some can be brilliantly colored at certain times of the year or at certain stages of their life cycles.

• • • • • • • FERNS • • • • • • • •

Ferns are found all over the eastern United States. Because the different species are so similar, they will be discussed here only as a group. If you want to know more about specific ferns, your local library or garden center should have a fern reference book.

Ferns have a unique life cycle, most of which we don't even see. They go through two stages: the ferns produce spores, which are microscopic, round fruiting bodies dispersed by the wind that land on the soil. The spores then produce the fern plant.

Ferns normally require moisture to grow, although the bracken fern can survive in a drier area if it does not get much direct sunlight. They all need shade. Ferns grow from an underground network of rhizomes and die back down to the ground each year. When they first start growing in the springtime, the unfurling fern leaf looks like the end of a fiddle and is called a fiddlehead.

You can identify ferns by the number of times that the leaves are dissected: once cut, twice cut, or three times cut. The bracken fern is three times cut. It normally grows up to about three feet tall. The other common fern is only once cut. It remains green at Christmas time, so it is called the Christmas fern.

• • • • • • • MOSSES • • • • • • • •

Mosses are probably one of the most abundant plants we find in our yards. The different types appear very similar; they normally produce a plush green mat of material. They grow on almost any surface where there is water available: on the ground, rocks, trees, and even lawn furniture if it has been sitting around for quite a while. Mosses help hold soil in place and break down rocks.

Mosses lack true roots and stems. They attach themselves with hairlike structures to rock, soil, and trees and have simple stalks instead of stems. These stalks cannot carry water to the leaves, so the leaves must get their moisture individually. The leaves do not have veins as do most of the plants in our yards. Most mosses are only a couple of inches tall, although some of the aquatic mosses can grow to lengths of several feet. Each moss clump contains both male and female plants; the sperm swims to the female moss during times of dew or rain. After fertilization a spore-producing appendage called the capsule stalk is formed on the female. The capsule bursts open when mature and the spores produce new male and female plants.

The easiest ways to tell the mosses apart are by their size, leaf shape, and color, and by the size and shape of the capsule and how it opens to release the spores. Habitat is also an identifier because some mosses like rocks, some like acid soils, and some like alkaline soils.

Wall Moss
page 135

Wall moss is a common moss that grows on rocks and walls. It rarely gets to be more than one inch tall. The stalks that produce the spores are quite long and spindly and culminate in a pointed spore capsule. If you look closely at the leaf tips you will notice a hairlike structure extending from the leaf. This is very characteristic of the wall moss and is probably used as a means of water conservation.

Star Moss
page 135

Star moss is a common moss that lives in fairly moist areas. It is often found on rotting wood or wood chips. It prefers a shady habitat but can also grow in subdued sunlight.

The star moss is about 1 to 1 1/2 inches tall. The leaves are oval, erect, and somewhat shiny. The endmost leaves form a whorled rosette that looks like a star; the other leaves are found in two rows along the stem. The fruiting or reproductive capsules hang down at the end of the stem. They are elongated and egg-shaped, rather like a kiwi fruit with a point on the end.

Feather Moss

Feather moss is a common moss of the forest; it especially likes to grow on tree trunks. It is normally found from the Appalachians in Georgia northward. Feather moss looks like a feather that has been ruffled up. It is short and stocky; the entire plant rarely grows more than two or three inches long. The leaves are very short, less than one-quarter inch.

Pincushion Moss

Pincushion moss is usually found in more acidic soil, often in sandy areas such as dunes along the Great Lakes or the Atlantic coastline. It grows right on the ground in very dense mats, frequently in small patches much like green pincushions. These patches can be anywhere from a few inches to many feet across. The pincushion mosses are generally light green or gray-green rather than the dark green color of most mosses. The plant, usually less than one inch tall, produces a small stalk with a pointed spore capsule that often grows two or three inches above the rest of the moss.

Tree Moss

As its name indicates, tree moss grows across the ground and its stems stand erect and branch out like tiny trees. The plant gets no higher than two to three inches tall. It grows in clumps so it may look like a miniature forest on the ground. If you look closely at the leaves you will see they have tiny teeth at the end. Tree moss normally requires moist conditions so it is not found in the drier parts of North America. The spore capsule grows to be about 1 1/2 inches long and comes to a small point.

Purple Moss and Silver Moss
page 135

The purple moss, sometimes called the burned ground moss, can be found all over the eastern United States except for the very southern states that border the Gulf of Mexico. This moss is generally less than one inch high. It can be very thick, giving it a carpetlike look. The narrow leaves curve under the main stem and have red bristles at the end. The

Purple Moss and
Silver Moss,
continued

spore capsule at the end of the stem usually points horizontally. These capsules can be purplish to red in color, and if they are predominant they give the whole mossy blanket a purplish sheen. This moss can withstand dry weather better than some of the other mosses. It therefore grows in places where the other mosses may not be found. During the dry periods the purple moss becomes quite brown, as if it had been burned; when rain comes it greens up again.

The silver moss is quite short, usually less than one-half inch tall. It is a silvery gray-green color. The short, oval leaves clasp the stem making a thick bed of green vegetation. The spore-producing capsules on the stalk hang downward much like a shepherd's staff. Silver moss is found all over the eastern United States and is common along walkways or anyplace there is a bit of land that is not cultivated. Though it looks similar to the pincushion moss, the silver moss has bigger beds.

• • • • • • **LIVERWORTS** • • • • • • •

Liverworts are related to mosses. They have fairly large leaves that spread out and attach themselves to the rock, tree, or wall they are growing on. These flattened leaves hug and take on the shape of the structure on which they are living. They normally need to grow where there is quite a bit of moisture available. Often liverworts will grow along with mosses and ferns in a shaded wet area.

Common Liverwort
page 136

Common liverwort has relatively fat leaves that spread out with fingerlike projections. It can be likened to a black hand with flattened, stubby fingers. These fingers represent the lobes of the liverwort leaf. The liverworts produce male and female plants. Tiny umbrellalike appendages produce the mating spores and sporophytes, or spore-producing bodies. The common liverwort leaf grows to be about one-half inch wide and up to two or three inches long. It is quite beautiful when covering an entire rocky hillside or wall.

• • • • • • • LICHENS • • • • • • •

A lichen is a symbiotic relationship of two types of plants, a fungus and an alga. In symbiosis two organisms live together for their mutual benefit. In this case the fungus provides the place for the alga to live and the alga produces food that nourishes the fungus. Lichens can grow on just about any surface and prefer moist, shady areas. The following three types are the most prevalent.

Crustose Lichen

Crustose lichens are very flat and are normally attached to rock or some hard material. The fibers may even grow into cracks and embed themselves there. If you were to run your fingernail across a crustose lichen, you would not feel any kind of an edge because the entire plant is attached to the substratum. These lichens can be brightly colored, especially in very wet climates.

Foliose Lichen
page 136

Foliose lichen is often called dog lichen or dog tripe. It is attached to its growing surface at only one spot. It is somewhat leafy but does not stand very erect off the tree or rock. A common foliose lichen is the shield lichen. It is pale green or gray. It is usually found on trees and logs in a deep forest where not much sunlight reaches it. Shield lichens can get to be about six inches across.

Fruticose Lichen
page 136

This lichen produces a fruiting body that grows up from a stalk. The most common of these are the pixie cup and the British soldier. The pixie cup has a tiny cup rather like a golf tee at the top of the stalk. It can be green, gray, or silver.

The British soldier has a gray to gray-green or silver stalk, on top of which grow flattened clublike structures that are bright red in color. Both the pixie cups and the British soldiers grow in clusters of six or seven to thirty or forty stalks. They seldom get to be more than one inch tall.

The fungus family, which includes the mushrooms, is made up of plants that are not green and do not flower. They are probably the most commonly distributed plants throughout the world. They can be various shapes and sizes; many are edible but others are quite poisonous.

The mushrooms we see in our yards are the fruiting bodies of a larger plant or network of plant cells called mycelium. This is a very complex network of fibers that take nutrients from dead organic material; because mushrooms do not contain chlorophyll and therefore cannot manufacture their own food, this is the only way they can survive. The function of the mushrooms is to produce the spores that propagate the underground mycelium. Because the actual plant is beneath the soil, picking the mushrooms does little harm to the plant, although if you pick them all not many spores will be produced and there will be fewer mushrooms in that area the following season. Mushrooms will grow on any dead organic material. They begin with a small bud and grow up into a mushroom over a period of days or weeks.

Different mushroom species are present at different times of year. Some of them grow in the early springtime, such as the morels; others grow during the summer, such as meadow mushroom; and a good number of them, such as the puffballs, grow during the wet, cool fall rains. All of them require a goodly amount of moisture to germinate and grow.

The identifying features of mushrooms are the cap, the stalk, the gills found underneath the cap, and the spores and spore prints. To make a spore print, place the mushroom cap gill side down on a piece of paper for twenty-four hours. This allows the spores to fall and make a pattern on the paper.

If in doubt about the identity of a mushroom, play it safe and don't pick it. You should also be very cautious about eating mushrooms with other types of food, especially alcohol, because a catalytic reaction can occur that is painful or even fatal. There are numerous field guides available that deal with mushrooms, some of which are listed in the bibliography.

Fairy Rings
page 137

Many people call any mushroom that grows in a circle a fairy ring, but the name actually refers to a particular species. Fairy rings normally appear in a circle, and as the mycelium grows the circle gets increasingly larger. This mushroom gets from about 2 to 2^1/$_2$ inches tall and the cap about ^{3}/$_4$ to 1^1/$_4$ inches across. The cap is smooth on the top. The gills are quite far apart and are white until the fungus is mature, when they turn brown or black. Most often the cap is light brown or pale buff. The fairy ring usually grows in grassy areas and appears in early spring and early fall when wet weather is prevalent. The spore print of this mushroom is white and therefore needs to be taken on dark paper.

Shaggy Mane
page 137

The shaggy mane is one of the inky caps. It can grow from two to four inches tall and has a scaly covering on the cap. The cap is narrow and pointed, almost thumblike in shape. This mushroom is most commonly found in the fall but it can grow any time of the year and in almost any open area where there is organic material available. Roadsides and city lots are likely places to find it.

Inky Cap
page 137

The inky cap is related to the shaggy mane although it does not get quite as tall, usually up to about three inches. The cap is rounder and has some scales on it, though not as many as does the shaggy mane. As the mushroom matures it begins to digest itself, turning into an inky mass of liquid.

Both the inky cap and the shaggy mane are a light gray to brownish gray on the top. The inky cap can grow anyplace there is organic material such as in lawns, city lots, and woodlands, and it grows in both spring and fall.

Haymaker Mushroom
page 137

Haymaker mushrooms grow about one to two inches tall. They are commonly found in lawns, fields, and pastures where there is grass growing. They are bell-shaped with fine grooves radiating from the center of the cap. The stalks are slender, white, and relatively fragile. The gills are brown and the mushroom is smooth and brown. Haymaker mushrooms normally grow in little groupings or clusters. The spore print is a pretty gray-brown.

Meadow Mushroom or Pink Bottom
page 137

The meadow mushroom grows from about two to four inches tall. The cap is white until it gets older, when it turns brown. The stalk is also white. The gills of the mushroom are pink and become brown as they mature. The spore print is a dark reddish brown.The meadow mushroom grows most commonly in late summer and early fall, especially during times of high precipitation. It is a common mushroom of pastures and open fields. The meadow mushroom may grow in a circle much like the fairy ring.

Puffball
page 137

Puffballs are probably the easiest common mushroom to identify. They are normally white, roundish in shape, and from one inch up to twelve inches or more in width. The surface of most puffballs is smooth but frequently becomes a little scaly as they get older. Puffballs are easiest to identify when they are young because of their white color. They usually grow from midsummer to fall; autumn is the preferred time in the northeastern United States. Most puffballs grow on the ground although some may grow on decaying wood.

As the mushroom matures, the outer shell breaks open and develops a hard leathery covering. This covering then opens and the spores leave the center of the puffball, usually dispersed by wind and rain. When raindrops hit the mushroom, puffs of spores come out. This gives the spores the best chance to grow because moisture is on the ground.

To positively identify a puffball, cut through it vertically. If it is not a puffball you will see a shape of a traditional mushroom in the cross section of the cut; if it is a puffball you will see a solid white interior.

Polypore Fungus or Shelf Fungus

Polypore fungus is easily identified because the underside of the cap has small holes or pores through which the spores escape. Most polypores grow on dead, rotting stumps or logs. They can range in size from a couple of inches to almost a foot across. Many call the polypores shelf fungi because they grow out horizontally from the tree like a shelf. The different varieties are usually named for their coloring, which can be white, gray, red, brown, or yellow.

Sulfur Polypore
page 137

The sulfur polypore is one of the more common polypores and is found growing on oak trees, especially those that have been recently cut and have had a chance to start decaying. Many call this the oak fungus. It is a sulfur yellow in color.

Many-colored Polypore
page 137

The many-colored polypore usually is fairly small, growing only about three inches tall. This fungus has many colors running in bands along the edge of the shelf—from browns to light greens, grays, oranges, and tans. The caps, which grow in colonies, usually overlap each other. It lives mostly on deciduous trees.

Artist's Fungus or Shelf Fungus
page 137

The artist's fungus is called shelf fungus as is the polypore. It grows on the sides of trees, particularly those that are dying or decaying. The hard, leathery upper portion can be brown or gray. The underside is white, but when injured with a fingernail or some kind of instrument it will turn brown. Some people have made drawings on it that remain for quite a number of years, hence the name artist's fungus.

Dead Man's Finger
page 137

Dead man's finger is classified as one of the carbon fungi. It is often found in lawns or at the edges of lawns or fields. It comes out of the ground in finger-like projections that appear to be made of a gray, skinlike material. Since these fingerlike projections are about the length of our fingers, up to three inches, and they grow in little clusters, many people have likened them to a dead man's hands sticking out of the ground.

Stinkhorn
page 137

The stinkhorn can vary dramatically in shape, color, and size. They can be orange, red, green, purple, or brown. The stinkhorns get their name because they produce a stalklike fruiting body covered with a material that smells atrocious enough to upset your stomach. This foul smell attracts flies and beetles, which carry the spore from one area to another. Some of the stinkhorns, especially the tall stalked ones, can grow from six to eight inches in height. The brightly colored species usually don't grow quite as tall, getting up to four or five inches.

Bird's Nest Fungus
page 137

Bird's nest fungi are small fungi found growing on dead and decaying matter such as branches. They are usually under one-half inch in length and one-quarter inch across. Inside the cuplike shape are the tiny "eggs," which are actually spore-containing capsules. These eggs burst open and spread the spores about. At certain stages of growth the eggs will not be easily evident. Taking into account the size, color, and texture of the bird's nest you can distinguish one type of bird's nest fungus from another.

Cup Fungus
page 136

As the name indicates this fungus has the shape of a cup. It is not very large, usually less than one inch in diameter and one inch or so tall. Many of these cups can be brightly colored. The two that are most prevalent are the orange fairy cup and the scarlet cup. We find both of these on rotting wood in woods, yards, and shrubby areas. The orange cup fungus is a bright orange both on the interior and exterior of the cup. The scarlet cup is bright red inside but has a gray to whitish exterior that accentuates the scarlet. As with most fungi, scarlet cups are not easily noticeable until they open up. Fungus spores can be carried good distances quickly; anytime there is a rainfall, within three days you may see either the orange fairy cup or the scarlet cup.

Ear Fungus
page 136

The ear fungus is one of the cup fungi that grow fairly erect to about an inch tall. It is light tan or brownish in color. This fungus grows in the moist rich soils of the deep forest and is fairly brittle. The "ear" is cylindrical and curved, and somewhat long. It reminds me more of a bat's ear than a human ear.

Jelly Fungus
page 136

When jelly fungus is dry it looks very much like a foliose lichen. It comes into being when rain or heavy dew is present; it takes on a great deal of water and becomes a slimy, jellylike mass. Most of these are found on branches of dead or dying trees and many are brightly colored.

The orange tremulo is a common jelly fungus. When it is dry it is a pale yellow; when water hits it, it becomes a bright orange. Other tremulos can range from white to brown to almost purple. Usually they do not grow much larger than a couple of inches.

Black jelly fungus is also very common, especially where there is water standing in swamps. Black jelly fungus is gray to black and lies flat against the bark of a tree or a branch. When rain or dew hits it, it absorbs all the moisture and become three to five times its size and quite jellylike in nature.

• • • • • • • SLIME MOLD • • • • • • • •

Slime molds are molds that seem to creep or flow along rather quickly for a plant and rather slowly for an animal. There have been discussions as to whether they should be considered a plant or an animal; most consider them plants because they have a stationary plantlike structure for most of their life cycle. Slime mold will start to grow once the conditions become right, usually after a rainfall or during a very wet period. They move across logs or other dead organic material, probably in search of food. Slime molds can be quite colorful, though most of those we see in North American are brown. The one pictured is the brown stemonitis. It creeps over a fairly large area but rarely gets to be more than one-half to one inch tall. If you happen to come across a slime mold it is interesting to sit and watch as the amoebalike movement carries it over the surface.

APPENDIX

HOW TO CONSTRUCT BIRD HOUSES AND FEEDERS

The following four boxes are easy to make and suitable for many backyard birds. I constructed them of $7/8$-inch cedar and assembled them with six-penny finish nails and waterproof glue. See pages 138 to 140 for diagrams.

Tray Feeder

A Two roof pieces $19^1/2$ by $7^1/4$ inches with a 23-degree angle cut on the $19^1/2$-inch side.

B Two gable pieces $12^1/2$ by $2^1/2$ inches each, cut with a 23-degree angle.

C Four $1/2$-inch dowels cut to 7 inches long.

D Two tray end pieces $17^3/4$ by $1^1/2$ inches.

E Two tray side pieces $17^3/4$ by $1^1/2$ inches.

F Tray bottom 16 by $11^1/4$ inches.

Oriole Feeder

A Two roof pieces 5 by $5^1/2$ inches with a 45-degree angle cut on the $5^1/2$-inch side. The roof pieces are centered over the face piece.

B Face piece 5 by $8^3/4$ inches with a 45-degree angle at the top. Two $3/8$-inch holes are drilled 3 inches apart.

C A $3/8$-inch dowel 5 inches long is sharpened on both ends and mounted halfway through the top hole.

D A $3/8$-inch perch dowel 5 inches long is mounted halfway through the bottom hole.

E A large screw eye is screwed into the roof on an angle so the threads are fixed firmly into one roof board.

Orange halves are placed on the sharpened dowel ends to attract orioles and other birds.

Wren House

A   Two roof pieces 5 1/2 by 6 inches with a 45-degree angle cut on the 6-inch side.

B   Two side pieces 5 by 6 inches are assembled flush with the bottom and a ventilation gap is left at the top.

C   Two end pieces 6 7/8 by 3 3/4 inch with a 45-degree angle cut at the top. One end piece has a 1 1/8-inch hole drilled 4 1/4 inches up from the bottom.

D   Bottom piece 3 3/4 by 3 3/4 inches with the corners cut off for drainage.

E   A large screw eye is screwed into the roof on an angle so the threads are firmly affixed to one roof board.

Nesting Roost

A   Back is 7 3/4 by 9 3/4 inches with a 70-degree angle cut on one of the 9 3/4-inch edges.

B   Top is 7 3/4 by 10 1/4 inches.

C   Two sides are 7 3/8 by 10 1/4 inches. A gentle curve is cut along the front 1 3/8 inches up from the bottom.

D   Front edge piece is 1 3/8 by 9 3/4 inches.

E   Bottom is 5 1/4 by 8 inches.

This box is used for nesting in the summer, especially by robins, and doubles as a small feeding station in the winter.

BIBLIOGRAPHY

Angier, Bradford. *Field Guide to Edible Wild Plants*. Harrisburg, Pennsylvania: Stackpole Books, 1974.

———. *Field Guide to Medicinal Wild Plants*. Harrisburg, Pennsylvania: Stackpole Books, 1978.

Audubon Society. *Master Guide to Birding*. New York: Alfred A. Knopf, 1983.

———. *Master Guide to Birding, vol. 1: Loons to Sandpipers*. New York: Alfred A. Knopf, 1983.

———. *Master Guide to Birding, vol. 2: Gulls to Dippers*. New York: Alfred A. Knopf, 1983.

———. *Master Guide to Birding, vol. 3: Old World Warblers to Sparrows*. New York: Alfred A. Knopf, 1983.

Borror, Donald J. and Richard E. White. *A Field Guide to the Insects*. Peterson Field Guides. Boston: Houghton Mifflin, 1970.

Brown, Lauren. *Grasslands*. Audubon Society Nature Guides. New York: Chanticleer Press, 1947.

Burt, William H. *Mammals of the Great Lakes Region*. Michigan: The University of Michigan Press, 1972.

Burt, William H. and Richard P. Grossenheider. *A Field Guide to the Mammals*. Peterson Field Guides. Boston: Houghton Mifflin, 1976.

Carr, Anna. *A Gardener's Guide to Common Insect Pests*. Emmaus, Pennsylvania: Rodale Press, 1978.

Conant, Roger. *A Field Guide to Reptiles and Amphibians of Eastern and Central North America*. Peterson Field Guides. Boston: Houghton Mifflin, 1975.

Dickerson, Mary C. *The Frog Book: North American Toads and Frogs*. New York: Dover Publications, 1969.

Durrell, Gerald. *A Practical Guide for the Amateur Naturalist*. New York: Alfred A. Knopf, 1982.

Ehrlich, Paul R., David S. Dobkin, and Darryl Wheye. *The Birder's Handbook: A Field Guide to the Natural History of North American Birds*. New York: Simon & Schuster, 1988.

Harrison, Hal H. *Wood Warblers' World*. New York: Simon & Schuster, 1984.

———. *A Field Guide to Birds' Nests*. Peterson Field Guides. Boston: Houghton Mifflin, 1975.

Holman, J. Alan, James H. Harding, Marvin M. Hensley, and Glen R. Dudderar. *Michigan Snakes: A Field Guide and Pocket Reference*. Michigan: Michigan State Museum, 1979.

Klots, Alexander B. *Field Guide to the Butterflies of North America, East of the Great Plains.* Peterson Field Guides. Boston: Houghton Mifflin, 1951.

Knopf, Alfred A. *Field Guide to North American Butterflies.* The Audubon Society Series. New York: Alfred A. Knopf, 1981.

——. *Field Guide to North American Mushrooms.* The Audubon Society Series. New York: Alfred A. Knopf, 1981.

——. *Field Guide to North American Reptiles & Amphibians.* The Audubon Society Series. New York: Alfred A. Knopf, 1979.

——. *Field Guide to North American Trees.* The Audubon Society Series. New York: Alfred A. Knopf, 1980.

——. *Field Guide to North American Wildflowers.* The Audubon Society Series. New York: Alfred A. Knopf, 1979.

Martin, Alexander C. *Weeds.* A Golden Guide. Racine, Wisconsin: Western Publishing Company, 1972.

McKnight, Kent H. and Vera B. *Mushrooms.* Peterson Field Guides. Boston: Houghton Mifflin, 1987.

Mitchell, John Hanson. *A Field Guide to Your Own Back Yard.* New York: W. W. Norton, 1985.

Mitchell, Robert T. *Butterflies and Moths.* A Golden Guide. Wisconsin: Western Publishing Company, 1977.

National Geographic Society. *Field Guide to the Birds of North America.* Washington: National Geographic Society, 1983.

Niering, William A. *Wetlands.* The Audubon Society Nature Guides. New York: Alfred A. Knopf, 1985.

Parsons, Frances Theodora. *How to Know the Ferns: A Guide to the Names, Haunts, and Habits of our Common Ferns.* New York: Dover Publications, 1961.

Perterson, Roger Tory. *A Field Guide to the Birds East of the Rockies.* Peterson Field Guides. Boston: Houghton Mifflin, 1980.

Perterson, Roger Tory, and Margaret McKenney. *A Field Guide to Wildflowers of Northwestern and North-Central North America.* Peterson Field Guides. Boston: Houghton Mifflin, 1968.

Reader's Digest. *North American Wildlife.* New York: Reader's Digest, 1982.

Robbins, Chandler S., Bertel Bruun, and Herbert S. Zim. *A Guide to Field Identification: Birds of North America.* Racine, Wisconsin: Western Publishing Company, 1966.

Shuttleworth, Floyd S. *Mushrooms and other Non-Flowering Plants.* A Golden Guide. Racine, Wisconsin: Western Publishing Company, 1987.

Smith, Alexander H. *The Mushroom Hunter's Field Guide.* Michigan: University of Michigan Press, 1971.

Smith, Miranda, and Anna Carr. *Rodale's Garden Insect, Disease and Weed Identification Guide.* Emmaus, Pennsylvania: Rodale Press, 1988.

Stokes, Donald and Lillian. *The Hummingbird Book.* Boston: Little, Brown, 1989.

Taylor, Norman. *Taylor's Guide to Trees.* Boston: Houghton Mifflin, 1988.

———. *Taylor's Guide to Gardening.* Houghton Mifflin, 1988.

Terres, John K. *The Audubon Society Encyclopedia of North American Birds.* New York: Alfred A. Knopf, 1980.

Zim, Herbert S. and Alexander C. Martin. *Flowers: A Guide to Familiar American Wildflowers.* A Golden Nature Guide. New York: Simon & Schuster, 1950.

———. *Trees: A Guide to Familiar American Trees.* A Golden Nature Guide. New York: Simon & Schuster, 1956.

Zim, Herbert S. and Hobart M. Smith. *Reptiles and Amphibians: A Guide to Familiar American Species.* A Golden Nature Guide. New York: Simon & Schuster, 1953.

ASSOCIATIONS

National Audubon Society. 950 Third Avenue, New York, NY 10022

National Wildlife Federation. 1412 16th Street NW, Washington, DC 20036

Nature Society. Griggsville, IL 62340

North American Bluebird Society. Box 6295, Silver Spring, MD 20916-6295

Purple Martin Conservation Association. Edinboro University of Pennsylvania, Edinboro, PA 16444